The Truth About Clutter

Why Am I Holding On To This?

Sue Anderson, CPO®,

Certified Professional Organizer and
CEO of Simplified Living Solutions, Inc.

Copyright

Dedication

This book is dedicated to all of Simplified Living Solutions' wonderful clients, each of whom had to bravely fight past their fears, insecurities and feelings of shame before even picking up the phone to call us for help in the first place. I applaud them for being vulnerable enough to allow my team and myself into their homes, offices and lives to help them declutter and get organized. I thank them for the trust they bestowed upon us and for allowing us to be an intimate part of their personal journey!

Contents

Introduction

Do you ever wonder why you hold on to things (or several of the same thing for that matter)? Or why it's so hard to let go of them? Have you ever felt embarrassed, ashamed or defeated by your clutter or excess? Do you wonder why tackling your clutter leaves you feeling frustrated, overwhelmed and paralyzed?

We'll answer those questions and more by exploring the psychology, feelings, emotions and reasoning behind *why* we have such a *strong* attachment to our stuff and *why* it's so difficult to let go of it. We'll take an honest look at what clutter *really* is and dig into how it sneaks into our lives and spaces without much help from us, and then stacks up until we're left feeling completely submerged and powerless. We'll take a look at the *damaging effects* clutter has on our lives and the real costs associated with holding on to things long after the value they bring to our lives is gone.

Once we spend some time understanding why we hold on to our stuff so tightly and how that is hurting us, we will explore the freeing power of letting go. You'll be provided with practical tips, action steps and information throughout to help you declutter and let go of those things that no longer serve a purpose and have been holding you down.

In addition to the experience, practical tips and knowledge that I share throughout the book, I have included numerous personal stories and firsthand accounts of struggles from some of the hundreds of clients I have worked with to help you better understand and apply these new concepts and ideas to your own lives and situations. Since the book doesn't have to be read sequentially, feel free to personalize your journey through the contents by reading the chapters in whatever order you'd like.

My desire to write this book stems from my lengthy experience as a certified professional organizer and a strong desire to educate, empower and motivate you to tackle (and defeat) your clutter and disorganization so that you can live a more powerful life. **I strongly believe that each one of us was created with a unique and powerful purpose for our lives and that excess clutter is keeping many people from being all that they could be.**

Getting organized is a journey, not an event. It takes time, persistence, effort and patience. If you apply all of the information and practical tips provided in this book, you will better understand *why* you've kept stuff and therefore have an easier time letting go of it. Decluttering will bring you one step closer to living out your life to the fullest. Let's get started!

Chapter 1:
What is Clutter?

"Clutter is not just physical stuff. It's old ideas, toxic relationships and bad habits. Clutter is anything that does not support your better self."

– Eleanor Brownn, Writer and Coach

After I carefully navigated my car around the bikes, balls and fallen trash cans that littered the driveway, Jenny sheepishly greeted me at the door for our initial meeting. As most of my clients do, she immediately began apologizing for what I was about to see. She followed her apologies with a string of reasons why she should have been able to do a better job of keeping up with things herself but wasn't able to.

As I reassured her that I had seen it all before and that I wasn't easily intimidated, I could see her breathe a sigh of relief. She smiled as I applauded her for fighting past her fears and shame to call me for help in the first place. And I watched all of the tension in her body disappear when I assured her that I could help her.

Gazing around the entryway and adjoining living room as we talked, I could see dishes from dinner the night before dangling precariously on the edge of laundry basket that had spilled over. Two or three boxes that were still not unpacked from their move a year earlier were now covered with dishes and food wrappers. Unopened mail and paperwork were strewn about on the floor, furniture and any other flat surface in the room.

As Jenny and I toured her home, we carefully calculated each step to avoid tripping over the toys, books, extra decor and other things that blocked our path. Excess electrical cords and tools were scattered here and there throughout the home. Since the time had not been taken to assign a home for her belongings, things were just left wherever they were last used. Without determining places where the stuff would be stored, there was also no way of limiting or monitoring the quantity of stuff she had because she couldn't clearly see exactly what was there, or how many of each item there were.

Working together, we sorted all of her belongings into categories and purged the excess. Left with only the items she needed, used or loved, we assigned homes for each category to live in. We set up rules and systems that would help her maintain the space and continue to limit the amount of stuff she held on to in each category.

Before we can understand *why* we hold onto clutter, we must first understand what it is. **Clutter is *anything* that takes up space in your life (physically or mentally) but doesn't serve a purpose, move you closer to your ultimate goals or add any value to your life. It's *anything* that you no longer need, use or love.** Clutter is *anything* that you have too much of, anything that you aren't really using for the purpose you originally intended and anything that is not serving your best interest. And it's *anything* that is clogging up your life or space and preventing you from being all you could be.

When we hear the word "clutter," we immediately picture a house that has been overtaken by too much physical stuff. While this image is an accurate representation of clutter, and the way most of us identify with it, the truth is that there are many different types of clutter besides just stuff. We can have clutter in several areas of our lives. While there are many types, this chapter offers an overview of the most obvious kinds and the ones that impact us the most. We'll delve a little deeper into each type of clutter in the chapters that follow.

Physical Clutter

Physical clutter is what we normally think of when we hear the word clutter. It's any material thing or belonging that you no longer need, use or love. The item(s) may have served a purpose or had value to you in your life before, but they no longer do.

Having too much stuff around that doesn't support our *current* goals or interests keeps us distracted from what we should be focusing on and keeps us stuck in the past. If you value hanging out with friends and family but your surroundings are filled with broken toys from your youth, unfinished projects and excess stuff — that leaves little space for entertaining.

Time Clutter

Time clutter is when your time is spent doing things that don't bring you any closer to your goals or the things that matter most to you in your life. Your schedule and your days are packed full of things to do that don't bring any value to your life or meet your needs.

Time clutter can also be when you have more appointments scheduled than the amount of time you have available for those appointments. This cuts into your downtime or family time. If you value family time, your spirituality and staying fit but your schedule is full of work commitments, networking events to grow your business and your favorite TV shows, then that leaves little time for hanging out with your family, attending church or going to the gym.

Mental Clutter

Mental clutter is when your mind is filled with past hurts or regrets and when it's busy trying to remember too many things at once. We tend to unknowingly take on too many responsibilities and then spend a lot of time and energy trying to balance everything in our minds.

Mental clutter robs you of clear and focused thinking. You are repeatedly reminded that you're not getting enough done and that you're not good enough. You're convinced you've got to work harder and faster and do things better.

Relationship Clutter

Relationship clutter is when you invest time and energy on relationships that don't bring any value to your life or people who don't have your best interests in mind. In most cases, they drain you of energy, confidence and motivation, which invariably pulls you further away from your goals and what you value most in your life.

These are the people whom you spend time with because you feel like it's what you *should do*, what you *have to do* or what *they* need you to do. They are the people in your life who only take from you and don't add any value to your life. The relationship benefits them, not you.

Visual Clutter

Visual clutter is when there are an excessive amount of things crowded together in chaotic order within your view.

It competes for your attention and pulls your mind and energy away from your focus on the task at hand. It serves as a constant visual distraction from those things in your life that you should be focusing on or that matter most.

CLUTTER TRUTH #2:
Borrow items you seldom use.

One way to combat clutter is to borrow items that you don't use very often. You don't have to buy every single thing – especially if you only need it once.

Food Clutter

Food clutter is when you eat more food than is necessary to nourish your body, or when you fill your diet with food and drink that you don't need and your body can't use. It's when you consume an excessive amount of things that do not serve your body properly, or add any value to it *or* your energy level.

The results of *food clutter* are being overweight, not feeling well, health issues, low motivation and self-loathing.

Remember, clutter is *anything* that you have too much of or that is not serving your best interest. It's *anything* that takes up space in your life physically or mentally but doesn't provide any value to your life. Clutter is anything you don't need, use or love. It is those things that you aren't really using for the purpose you originally intended. ***Clutter is anything that clogs up your life and prevents you from being all you could be.***

Now that you have an overview of the main types of clutter, we'll dig a little deeper into each kind in the following chapters.

It's your turn...

FOOD FOR THOUGHT:

Right now, can you think of anything that is clutter in your life — but you hadn't realized it before?

ACTION STEP:

1. Pick a room to focus on in your home or your office.
2. Set a timer for 15 minutes.
3. Grab an empty box or trash bag.
4. Identify those things that you readily know you can live without and place them into the box or bag.
5. (Repeat as frequently or long as you'd like if you have time and a desire to do so.)
6. Immediately place box or bag in your car so that you can drop it off at your local charity the next time you're out.

RULES FOR SUCCESS:

1. Take donations all of the way to your car rather than simply placing them by the door. (Many times bagged donations languish in people's homes for years.) Once you make the decision something can go, it needs to GO.
2. Make it easy on yourself and drop everything off at one place. In all honesty, most people want to make sure their unwanted stuff lands in the hands of the perfect person that needs it. But, the reality is that the majority of us won't set the time aside to deliver everything to the specific places, resulting in the unnecessary stuff never leaving our homes or offices. Trust that the stuff you let go of will end up in the hands of the person that truly needs it – and let it go!

Chapter 2:
Physical Clutter

"Trying to be happy by accumulating possessions is like trying to satisfy hunger by taping sandwiches all over your body."

– George Carlin, Author, Actor and Comedian

Physical clutter is what we normally think of when we hear the word clutter. The Oxford dictionary defines clutter as *a collection of things lying about in an untidy mass.* That is an extremely vague definition and leaves out the most relevant component – excess. Having things lying about in an untidy mass simply suggests a messy space, not necessarily a cluttered one. Our spaces are really only considered cluttered when there is *too much* stuff.

Clutter consists of an overabundance of material things, objects or belongings that you don't need or use. The item(s) may have served a purpose or had value for you in your life before, but they no longer do. Clutter also means having an excessive amount of the same type of thing, so much so that you could never use, wear or need all of them.

Another extremely common characteristic of *physical clutter* is having more stuff than you have space to store it in. When your belongings begin to invade and take over your living spaces, rendering them unusable for their implied purpose, your stuff is then classified as clutter because of its excessiveness.

The great majority of our clients call because they have literally lost the use of a room, a basement, a garage – or an entire house – because of their excessive clutter. Many times people lose control of their homes or offices when they go through life-changing transitions such as a serious illness, marriage, divorce, birth of a child, death of a loved one or merging households, to name a few.

CLUTTER TRUTH #3:

The prime real estate of any space should be used to house the things that you use most often, not your excess.

Prime real estate refers to the area of any given space that is easiest to access with the least amount of movement and effort from you. In the kitchen, the prime real estate would be the cabinets that are at eye level. In the bedroom, the prime real estate would be the top drawers of your dresser. In the bathroom, it would be the medicine cabinet.

These life-changing transitions come with their own set of obligations, consequences and emotional responses that distract us from the influx of stuff that continues to sneak into our home, office and life. By the time we realize we have lost control of our surroundings, it's too late and we're left feeling powerless.

Many times as we are transitioning, we begin acquiring new things that go with the change, like stuff for our new baby, our new spouse's belongings, or medical supplies and equipment for an illness. At the same time, we're not ready to say goodbye to many aspects of our old life and so we hang on to the stuff that went with it even though it doesn't support our new life.

Because she was a wife and a busy mom to 8-year-old Wyatt, Lindsay's house was always somewhat cluttered and disorganized. She and her husband Bill would tackle the excess stuff every year or so and weed out and donate the things Wyatt had outgrown or no longer played with. The clutter and disarray minimally impacted their lives.

That is, until Lindsay awoke in the middle of the night with an unbearable headache. The pain was so excruciating that it felt like her head was going to explode! After rushing to the hospital, they learned something that would change their lives forever.

Unbeknownst to any of them, Lindsay had a brain tumor. There had been absolutely no warning signs. The doctors performed emergency surgery that night to remove the tumor. After the surgery, Lindsay suffered from short-term memory loss, which made it next to impossible for her to stay on task or remember where things belonged.

By the time her concerned family called us in to help them take back control of the family home, clutter had overtaken the house. The family was left feeling unsure where to even begin. Since the brain tumor and emergency surgery had left Lindsay easily confused and unable to remember where things were, the family knew it was crucial that they call us in to help create order for her.

*When we arrived, every bedroom floor in the home was piled high with clothes, toys, trash, DVDs and other random objects. We quickly learned that Wyatt had outgrown most of the clothes in his dresser drawers and closets. **Because the drawers (the prime real estate*) were full of things he could no longer use, the stuff that he was using had no place to go.** Once we removed his outgrown stuff, there was plenty of space for his current stuff to be stored.*

*See Clutter Truth #3 for definition.

We found a similar situation in the parents'
bedroom – their drawers and closet (the prime real
estate) were full of things they weren't currently
using. *Once again, since their prime storage spaces*
were full of things they weren't using, there was no
place for their current stuff to go. Granted, the
bedroom was fairly small, as was the closet. The big
problem we found in this room was an excessive
number of t-shirts. There had to be close to 250 t-
shirts! They had literally taken over every nook and
cranny of available storage space in that room.

These t-shirts were no longer even being worn.
Lindsay and Bill were holding on to each and every
one of them for memory's sake and had plans to
make a t-shirt quilt out of them ***someday***.

In a home, your living spaces are considered the
prime real estate. Living spaces are the areas that
you spend the majority of your time in when you're
at the home – kitchen, living room, bedrooms and
the dining room. ***Items you are no longer using***
should never be kept in the prime real estate of
your living spaces. *Once we moved the t-shirts from*
the bedroom's prime storage spaces to tubs in the
basement where they belonged, we were able to
easily fit the stuff they were currently wearing into
the drawers and closet space.

After reorganizing Lindsay's entire home, we left everything labeled so that she would be able to easily navigate her way throughout her days at home.

CLUTTER TRUTH #4:

Set space limits for how much of any item you'll keep.

Make a standing decision about how much space any given item can have. Once you've filled the designated space, you cannot add more to it without letting go of others in order to open up the space needed for the new ones. For instance, you can only keep as many books as you can fit on your bookshelves. When you decide you want to keep some of your new books, your older books will have to go to make room for them.

Having too many physical belongings around that we don't need, use or love brings many consequences along with it. We'll explore those ramifications in greater detail in Chapter 9. Now we'll move on to the lesser known types of clutter.

It's your turn...

FOOD FOR THOUGHT:

We wear 20% of our clothes, 80% of the time.

ACTION STEP:

1. Choose your office or a room in your home to focus on.
2. Identify the *prime real estate* in that space. A few examples of what might be considered *prime real estate* in any given room are:
   a. Desk drawers in an office.
   b. Eye level cabinets in a kitchen, closet or pantry.
   c. Top dresser drawers in a bedroom.
3. Remove any items that you find in those spaces that are not needed or used frequently.
4. Re-fill the space with items that you *do* use frequently.

RULES FOR SUCCESS:

1. Things will get messier *during* the organizing process. There's no way around it! Your initial thought when you empty the prime real estate spaces in any area will undoubtedly be *what do I do with this stuff?* Fight past trying to figure that out for the moment. If necessary, put things in tubs and stack them until you can get back to them.
2. Don't store excess or back-up supplies in your prime real estate. For instance, in a desk drawer you should only have a couple of pens, white-out, a handful of paper clips and rubber bands, etc. as opposed to keeping all six boxes of paper clips and the entire package of pens. Keep only what you need in the prime real estate areas and store the surplus in an out of the way place.

Chapter 3:
Time Clutter

"The bad news is time flies. The good news is you're the pilot."

– Michael Altshuler, Coach and Speaker

Time clutter is when your time is spent doing things that don't bring you any closer to your goals or the things that matter most to you in your life. Excess is a main component of *time clutter*, just as it is with any type of clutter. It's when you fill your time with things you don't need to do or want to do, when you schedule more commitments than you have available time, and your days are packed full of things to do that don't bring any value to your life.

Time clutter also is a result of poor time management. When you schedule more commitments than you have available time for, you cut into the time that you could be spending focused on the things that you really *do* enjoy and that matter most to you in your life, as well as those things that bring you closer to your goals.

If you value hanging out with friends, getting a daily workout and growing your business but the majority of your time is spent lying on the couch watching TV, playing video games and immediately responding to every text, Facebook or Twitter alert you receive, then that leaves little time for the things that are the most important to you.

CLUTTER TRUTH #5:

When you overschedule your time, it cuts into your downtime.

Since time is something we can't physically see increasing or decreasing, it's easy to overschedule our time with things that look good on the surface but end up taking away from our downtime or self-care.

When my children were growing up, I battled with time clutter without even realizing it. We were constantly, and I mean constantly, running from one place to the next. We spent every single minute together on the go. Since we looked like every other busy family, nothing about our lives stood out as wrong to me.

As a single mom for the majority of my children's lives, I'd return home from work every night and fix a quick dinner. While I'm thankful that we would all sit down to dinner together and catch up with each other's day, I remember always having my eye on the clock to insure that we would finish eating in time to make it out of the house and to whatever commitment we had that day on time.

Because our time together was normally spent doing activities both of my children enjoyed, or things that we had to do like grocery or clothes shopping, it took me quite a while to realize that I had filled our time with things we didn't HAVE to be doing. One of my daughters was very involved in choir, Girl Scouts and basketball, while the other daughter participated in cheerleading, softball and D.E.C.A. (an organization that supports young entrepreneurs). Since we were a single-parent household, all three of us had to go along to each and every thing the other family member was involved in.

While I was thankful that my children's involvement with these activities kept them out of trouble, I began to realize our days were flying by at a very quick rate without much quiet downtime. There wasn't a lot of time spent resting or sitting still, alone with just our thoughts. Then, and only then, I realized that I had overfilled our time with things that didn't necessarily serve us well, even though they were positive and appeared to be what we wanted to do.

Once I realized what we were doing, I made it my goal to teach my children (and myself!) that it isn't necessary to constantly be on the go. The first step in changing this pattern (or any habit, for that matter) was to become highly aware of every decision I made about how we spent our time. I took the time to weigh out the good and bad of each activity we were participating in. Armed with this new information, I made the decision to reduce the number of after-school activities my girls were participating in from three to two. This one simple decision made all of the difference in the world and freed up the downtime we all needed. I was shocked to realize that my children weren't the least bit saddened by this decision!

CLUTTER TRUTH #6:

The first step of changing any habit is to increase your awareness of it.

When you're ready to make a change, it's important to increase your awareness of any habit or pattern that you want to change. When you do that, you also increase your awareness of how that habit or pattern impacts your life. Reflecting on the negative consequences and triggers of the habit helps to motivate you to take the time to map out how you can successfully make the change.

Spending our time doing things that don't bring us any closer to our goals or what matters most in our lives has a negative impact on our lives. We'll take a closer look at the impact it has on our lives in Chapter 10.

It's your turn...

FOOD FOR THOUGHT:

"Either you run the day, or the day runs you."
– Jim Rohn

ACTION STEP:

1. If you don't use a calendar, it's time to start. By putting your commitments down in writing, you're better able to see when you are overbooking yourself.
2. Take time to find the *right* calendar for you and your life. For some, an electronic calendar works best. Others may prefer a wall calendar. I personally use a paper planner with big squares for each day because I like being able to see an entire month at a glance.

RULES FOR SUCCESS:

1. Use only one calendar.
2. Write all appointments, sports schedules, birthdays, etc. on the calendar so you can quickly see any conflicts. When you put something on your calendar, you can toss the paper back-up because it no longer serves a purpose.
3. Don't simply clip scheduled appointment cards to the calendar. Take the time to enter the appointments into the date they are scheduled for and toss the reminder cards.

Chapter 4:
Mental Clutter

"Don't let yesterday use up
too much of today."

– Will Rogers, Actor and Humorist

As we've discussed in the preceding chapters, clutter comes in a variety of forms but always indicates excess. *Mental clutter* is no different in that respect. *Mental clutter* is when your mind is full of things you need to do, errands you need to run, things you're trying to remember, decisions you need to make and so on. We tend to take on too many responsibilities and then spend a lot of time and energy trying to balance everything in our minds.

Mental clutter is a big reason that organized people are always making lists. They do that because, by creating a list, you get all of that stuff out of your brain and dumped onto paper, thereby freeing up all of that brain space to be used for the bigger issues. Scribbling to-do lists on Post-It® Notes and then lining your desk with them until you no longer even notice them is not the way to create an effective to-do list, but that's a whole other book!

Past (or current) hurts or traumatic situations have a way of creeping back into our present life and haunting us or distracting us from what's important now. They crowd out the things our brains could be focused on in the here and now. *Mental clutter* robs you of clear and focused thinking. It repeatedly tells you that you're not getting enough done and that you're not good enough. You've got to work harder and faster and do things better.

We carry around guilt from our past about things that are better off forgotten. Our thoughts are filled with regret about the mistakes we've made, the people we've let down and the bad choice(s) we've made. Once again, these things have a way of creeping into our minds at the most inopportune times and distracting us from focusing on the here and now and the goals for our future.

Distractions are another great source of mental clutter. The *Oxford Pocket Dictionary of Current English* defines a distraction in one definition as *a thing that prevents someone from giving full attention to something else.* In another definition, distraction is described as *an extreme agitation of the mind or emotions.* With cell phones in almost every person's hands these days set to alert us to every single Facebook message, text message and email we receive, we are inundated with constant distractions that keep us from focusing on what's most important to us.

Our minds are constantly flooded with information and images we see online and on TV, movies, commercials and billboards. These subliminal messages suggest how we should think, how we should feel, what we should eat or wear, and much more. Our minds are overrun with this never-ending barrage of information.

CLUTTER TRUTH #8:
Silence or turn off alerts on your smartphone.

I know many of you just gasped when you saw this one! But to limit mental clutter and distractions, it is necessary to take back control of your attention. One of the best ways to do that is by disabling all of the alerts on your phone. You don't have to know (or respond) the instant someone sends you an email, likes your Facebook or Twitter post or texts you. Choose to check your phone for these things in less frequent intervals.

Worry and negative self-talk provide yet another source of *mental clutter*. We worry about what is going to happen, what has happened and about other what-if situations. The great majority of us have an almost constant dialogue of negativity going on in our minds about ourselves. We're constantly judging and critiquing our actions and thoughts.

Mental clutter leaves us in a constant state of fight-or-flight, which leads us to make bad decisions that impact our health and well-being. *Mental clutter* weighs us down as much, if not more, than *physical clutter*. We'll explore these and other consequences in greater detail in Chapter 11.

It's your turn...

FOOD FOR THOUGHT:

Imagine how much your creativity is stifled when your mind is constantly busy trying to hold on to and remember other things.

ACTION STEP:

1. Take some time to capture all of your thoughts on paper. Just keep writing until you feel that you've "released" everything from your brain.
2. Once you've done that, organize your thoughts into categories so that it will make it easier for you to act on them. You might group them into the following types of categories:
   a. Calls to make
   b. Errands
   c. Marketing ideas
3. Take action on the ones that need action. Determine a place to keep the other information that doesn't need immediate action. For instance, your marketing ideas could go in a folder labeled as such until you're ready to take action on it.
4. You will immediately feel a greater sense of control each time you do this exercise.

RULES FOR SUCCESS:

1. It's imperative that you not only jot down your thoughts and to-do's, but rather that you take time to organize that information in a useful manner as well. Having piles and piles of unorganized to-do lists isn't helpful. Since everything is just mixed together in no certain order, you are immediately left feeling dumbfounded and so you simply turn your attention elsewhere.

Chapter 5:
Relationship Clutter

"If you're brave enough to say goodbye,
life will reward you with a new hello."

— Paulo Coehlo, Author and Lyricist

When it comes to comparing how *relationship clutter* lines up with the definition of *physical clutter* that I shared in Chapter 2, you'll find it has more to do with investing your time and energy into something (in this case, someone) that doesn't bring any value to your life.

In fact, in most cases, they do just the opposite. They consume as much of you as you'll allow and offer you nothing in return. These relationships cause so much stress and adversity that they challenge your resilience on a regular basis. When you are involved in an abundance of these self-sacrificing relationships, we call that *relationship clutter.*

Many times (but not always), these types of relationships are formed, or allowed to continue, out of an unspoken obligation you feel. You may think that having a relationship with that person is what *you should do,* what *you have to do* or what *the other person needs you to do.*

Healthy relationships are created with a give-and-take connection where both parties feel supported and valued even though they maintain their independence. Granted, it is to be expected that there will be times when we play the stronger, nurturing, supportive role to someone who is hurting or struggling, but that should only be a portion of the relationship. It should not be the dynamic for the entire existence of the relationship.

CLUTTER TRUTH #9:

When you choose to spend time in a negative relationship, you forfeit using that time to create positive relationships instead.

Investing time and energy into relationships that don't add any value to your life comes at a cost. Choose to spend your time in relationships that rejuvenate and support you.

Filling our life and time with unhealthy relationships mentally drains us rather than recharging us. That is just one of the consequences of *relationship clutter.* We'll explore other consequences of *relationship clutter* in greater detail in Chapter 12.

It's your turn...

FOOD FOR THOUGHT:

"When you say 'yes' to others, make sure you are not saying 'no' to yourself." – Paulo Coehlo

ACTION STEP:

1. Spend some time tuning into your thoughts and feelings about your various relationships rather than continuing to ignore them. As it becomes clearer to you, begin pulling away from the friendships that simply drain you.
2. Move spending time with people you enjoy further up on your priority list. When you are a little more aggressive about lining up time with folks you like being with, that leaves less time for the undesirable relationships to creep in.

RULES FOR SUCCESS:

1. Don't guilt yourself into continuing a relationship that isn't feeding your spirit.

Chapter 6:
Visual Clutter

"You can't do big things if you're distracted by small things."

– Jairek Robbins, Speaker and Coach

Visual clutter is when there is an excessive amount of things crowded together in chaotic order within your view. It competes for your attention and pulls your mind and energy away from your focus on things at hand. It serves as a constant visual distraction from those things that matter most in your life.

CLUTTER TRUTH #10:

Organize smartphone and tablet apps into groups to minimize *visual clutter.*

You may not realize that when you look at your phone or tablet and it is covered from one end to the other with apps, it's stressful. Create folders to group the apps into – a game folder for games, a business folder for work related items, etc. This should clear your phone tremendously. Not only that, it should save you time by helping you find what you need quicker. You can duplicate the idea of creating folders to consolidate all of the things on your computer screen as well.

Naomi worked from home as a medical transcriptionist. Because she, her husband and two teenage daughters were already somewhat crammed into their small, two-bedroom house, she had to use a portion of the dining room to create her makeshift office. Her desk alone took up more than half of the space. As the clutter from her workspace exploded more and more, it eventually took over the family's eating area in the room.

Messiest Desk Contest – Before

We met Naomi when she was chosen as the winner of Simplified Living Solutions' Messiest Desk Contest. The prize was a free desk makeover. The "before" picture of her desk is a great example of visual clutter. Can you see all of the distractions you would have trying to work and concentrate in this area?

Just look at the number of Post-It® Notes hanging from the desk that are competing for her attention. Add to that the excess amount of pictures, knickknacks and other décor battling to be noticed. Books are piled up on the desk and falling over on the shelves. Paperwork is strewn about here and there in no specific order. You get the point.

Not only did Naomi's home office not provide a peaceful and productive environment to work in, it also affected her family each time they came into the dining room! As a matter of fact, all of the visual clutter created a great deal of stress, inattention and a lack of productivity. As you can guess, a lot of her time was spent searching for what she needed and being distracted by the other notes and paperwork that were clamoring for her attention as she tried to focus on the task at hand.

Messiest Desk Contest - After

The picture at the bottom of the previous page is of that same space after we decluttered and organized it. Isn't it peaceful? Can't you already see how much more productive you would be in this space? We removed some of the excess décor and knickknacks so that the ones that were left weren't disproportionate to the space and would get the attention they rightly deserved. In addition to creating an organized reference filing system, we created an action paperwork system for the papers that she was currently working on and needed to get to easily.

We gathered all of her books together and placed them upright in order of their height so that they flowed together well and were also easy to get at. The information from all of the Post-It® Notes was organized and placed into the red or blue reference binders in the bottom left cabinet. It's hard to see in the "before" picture, but there was a glass door in front of the shelves on the left originally. The door made the space behind it unusable because there were piles of stuff in front of the door, making it very difficult to access the stuff behind it. We simply removed the door so that things could easily flow in and out of that area. We also placed the pictures of things that motivated her underneath a plastic desk mat so that she could easily see them but also use that space to work.

Another great example of *visual clutter* is a
computer screen, smartphone or tablet that is
completely covered with icons. It's stressful just to
look at that – and then try to find the icon you
need! Icons can be organized and grouped into
folders, which would reduce the *visual clutter* and
also reduce your stress level.

Visual clutter can also be competing patterns in the
same space. If there are a variety of patterns, it is
difficult to visually process them all.

As mentioned before, *visual clutter* reduces your
effectiveness and productivity, which in turn affects
your bottom line. We'll explore the other
consequences of *visual clutter* in greater detail in
Chapter 13.

It's your turn...

FOOD FOR THOUGHT:

Sometimes things start blending into our scenery and we don't even notice them anymore. Take a look around you with a fresh set of eyes, noticing all of the things that you didn't see before.

ACTION STEP:

1. Gather all of the random sticky notes together that you have hanging on and around your desk.
2. Separate them into groups of like with like. For example, you may have several that have passwords on them. Or several that have frequently used phone numbers. And undoubtedly you'll find some with information you no longer need.
3. Obviously you should immediately toss or recycle the unnecessary notes. Transfer the information you still need onto a reference sheet that groups the various notes together in an organized manner, category by category.
4. If your reference sheet is just one or two pages long, you can store it in a hard sheet protector that you can tuck between books or hang somewhere so that you can quickly grab it when you need the information. If it is longer than just a couple of pages, use a small folder or binder of some type to house it.

RULES FOR SUCCESS:

1. Don't use an oversized binder to hold the reference sheet(s) because that will *consume* more storage space than necessary.
2. Make sure that however you store it, that it's still super easy to get to or it won't work.

Chapter 7:
Food Clutter

> "Take care of your body. It's the
> only place you have to live."
>
> – Jim Rohn, Author and Speaker

Food clutter is no different than any other clutter. Just as described in Chapter 2, the most relevant component of any clutter is excess. *Food clutter* is when you consume more food and drink than is necessary to nourish your body.

Another basic element of clutter is that it doesn't add value to your life. In the case of *food clutter,* it is when you fill your diet with an *excessive* amount of food and drink that *doesn't provide a valuable source of nourishment* for your body.

Having more stuff than you have space to store it in is another fundamental ingredient of clutter. *Food clutter* is no different in that your body begins to expand because you are consuming more food than your body can hold, process or use.

CLUTTER TRUTH #12:
Take time to plan your meals and snacks.

The key to success in any change is planning. Take time to prepare a plan and strategy to reach your goals. Prepare a healthy meal plan and grocery list weekly to reduce the temptation of grabbing your favorite fast-food meal.

What I've learned over the years is that we avoid the things we don't like to do, or aren't good at, by using the excuse that we don't have time to do it. Granted, sometimes we really don't have time to do the things we need to do, but many times we manage to squeeze in time to do the things we enjoy rather than the things we really should do.

While I absolutely love organizing and truly see the value in taking the time to get organized, I struggle in the area of food clutter. Why? Because I don't enjoy grocery shopping or cooking so I normally just don't get around to doing it. I tell myself other things are more important. Of course, the other "more important things" are the things I enjoy doing.

I feel like I spent my entire life being teased because I'm organized, especially when I was growing up. I'd hear things like, "She's O.C.D." and "She's a pitcher! She never holds on to anything." Even today, my clients constantly giggle at the level of excitement I have when I think about helping them get organized. I thoroughly enjoy every single step of the organizing process.

On the other hand, I don't enjoy cooking at all. I wasn't born with the innate ability to read a recipe and feel like I could taste it because I understood the ingredients so well. I've been told that people enjoy chopping up ingredients and playing around with recipes – ugh! Some have even gone as far as to say that chopping up ingredients is therapeutic for them. The thought of that being enjoyable is almost humorous to me! (Just as my enjoying the organizing process is to others.)

Since I am no longer responsible for preparing meals for my children because they are adults now, there is nothing that forces me to cook. It's so much easier and quicker just to order from a restaurant. That way I can get the eating out of the way so that I can get back to doing the things I enjoy. Unfortunately, this habit resulted in a tremendous weight gain for me. It wasn't that I was overeating as much as it was that I was eating things that weren't good for me. I allowed this to go on for years until I couldn't ignore the negative impact the weight gain had on my life.

Once I decided I had to do something to change this, I met with a coach who helped me figure out a healthy weekly menu. From there, we created a grocery shopping list. None of this process was fun for me at all! Even recounting it here for you, I can still feel how much I disliked it! As soon as we got through all of that, she dropped the bombshell – she said I'd have to set time aside for grocery shopping and meal prep. WHAT!?

It may seem that I'm being overly dramatic about this, but for me, that was a **huge** bombshell. She suggested that I spend one day a week pre-cooking meals for the week so that I could easily grab them when I was on the go or had limited time. Give up an entire day to cook – are you kidding me?

I had to keep my goal of losing weight and getting healthy in the forefront of my mind in order to dedicate my time and energy to doing something I detested. Thankfully, I did exactly as she instructed and successfully lost all of the excess weight. I was able to do that because my meals and snacks were prepared in advance and well-planned out, free from things that didn't provide nutrients for my body. I also didn't bring any unhealthy foods or snacks into my house that I might be tempted by.

I'm happy to report that after about a year of doing this week after week I can tolerate my cooking days much better. They still are far from enjoyable, but *they're not quite as painful as they used to be. **I also don't see them as a day I'm giving up, but rather as an investment in myself.***

CLUTTER TRUTH #13:
Avoid over-purchasing food you don't need just because it's on sale.

We're automatically conditioned to think that anything on sale is a great deal. We assume that we better act quickly and purchase it. But buying things you don't need just because they are on sale is not a sale at all! **You save 100% not buying things you don't need.**

When we consume an excessive amount of food that does not serve our body properly, it can result in being overweight, not feeling well, health issues, low motivation and self-loathing. We'll dig into these and other consequences in greater detail in Chapter 14.

It's your turn...

FOOD FOR THOUGHT:

Brad Plumer of *The Washington Post* reported that American families throw out between 14 and 25 percent of the food and beverages they buy – a phenomenon that can cost each household as much as $2,275 a year.

ACTION STEP:

1. Go through all of the food in your refrigerator, pantry or other storage area and systematically purge expired or stale foods.
2. Let go of those things that you thought you'd like but didn't.
3. Consolidate duplicate open items to free up more space.
4. Take a realistic look at the amount of each item you have and make an informed decision about whether or not you need that much. If you have five containers of cinnamon but only use cinnamon once a year when you bake cookies, wouldn't it be safe to say you don't need that much? Let the excess go.

RULES FOR SUCCESS:

1. Taking the time to group similar items together can help you make better educated decisions on what things to keep or let go of.
2. Store items that go together with each other to avoid overbuying things. For instance – since sugar, flour, brown sugar and baking soda are all used for baking, you can gather them together in one container for easy access and so you can quickly and accurately see how much of each item you have.

Chapter 8:
How Does Clutter Impact You?

"Clutter is not just the stuff on the floor. It's anything that stands between you and the life you want to be living."

– Peter Walsh, Professional Organizer,
Author, Television and Radio Personality

There are very real mental, physical, financial, spiritual and emotional consequences of having things in our lives that don't serve a purpose, or that no longer support who we are *currently.* Or better yet, who we *want to be.* Now that we know and understand what clutter is, we'll spend a little time in this chapter summarizing the negative impact clutter has on our lives and the many ways it lies to us. In the chapters that follow, we'll explore the negative cost of each type of clutter in more detail.

You may think that you can ignore clutter in your home, office or life and that it won't bother you, but nothing could be farther from the truth. **You can't ignore clutter because the truth of the matter is that** *clutter never shuts up! It's constantly talking to you* **– and it's never saying anything nice or positive. Rather, it belittles you by exaggerating the reality of the situation and fabricating lies about you.** When you have stuff around that you no longer need, use or love (or that doesn't support your current life or goals), that stuff is always screaming at you and reminding you of things you would be better off forgetting.

Clutter screams, "You're a loser!"

Clutter reminds you of all of the things you forgot to do, all of the things you screwed up, all of the times you were hurt and all of the times you lost someone you loved. It reminds you of when you were thinner, younger or better in some way. *Since clutter is always talking to you and reminding you of all of your failures, that constant negative dialogue leaves you feeling beaten down, defeated and depressed.* Additionally, it zaps any motivation you may have had to change the situation.

While helping Amanda declutter and organize her basement, I asked her thoughts about all of the stuff that was tucked behind a door that was causing it not to open fully. At first glance I had no idea what it was. She said that everything behind the door could go. As I began to pull it out, I could see that it was an easel with a chalkboard on one side and a white board on the other. There were several pieces to it.

Once I removed all of it, I pushed the door all of the way against the wall so that it was opened fully. The minute I did that Amanda exhaled deeply and said "I'm not only glad that the door opens fully now, but I'm also relieved that the easel is gone because every time I looked at it I felt bad for breaking it!" (Remember, clutter is always talking to us!)

CLUTTER TRUTH #14:
Take it one room at a time, one shelf at a time.

Thinking you can get your entire home or office organized in a day is impossible. A typical linen closet averages three hours to organize. Getting organized is a process that takes time and a lot of attention to detail. Break down the organizing task by picking an area and then splitting it into smaller chunks. A desk could be broken down by drawers. A linen closet can be broken down by shelves.

Clutter keeps you locked in yesterday

Songs and smells immediately trigger memories that take us back to a certain place and time. So does our stuff. Clutter can trigger memories and feelings from our past, both good and bad. All of these memories and feelings keep us distracted from the here and now. When we are surrounded by stuff from our past, we can't focus on our future and pursuing our dreams because we are constantly distracted by reminders of yesterday.

When your home or office is full of constant distractions and reminders of the past, your focus tends to get stuck on the past rather than the present. Not only can you not focus on the present with all of that stuff from your past hanging around, but you definitely can't give much thought to the future! When your space is full of stuff that doesn't support your *current life,* there is no open space available for the things to come in that bring you closer to your goals or to a fuller life.

Clutter affects your physical and mental health!

Surprisingly, clutter has a direct impact on your physical and mental health as well. The way our home and office look and work has a direct impact on how we feel and function. The constant negative chatter of a cluttered and disorganized home or workspace increases your stress level immensely.

Clutter is always there, distracting you from the task at hand and the things that are most important in your life. It puts an enormous amount of pressure on us by constantly reminding us of all the things we were supposed to do, but haven't. It weighs on you constantly and drains you mentally, physically, emotionally and spiritually. You're left feeling helpless, out of control, stressed out and anxious. Since there isn't a peaceful place to regroup, refresh or relax, the thinking part of your brain eventually just shuts off.

Stating the obvious, stress that is left unchecked can cause heart attacks, panic attacks, increased anxiety and high blood pressure, just to name a few issues. It also causes us to make poor decisions. In addition, the more material things you have strewn about, the higher your risk is for tripping or falling over that stuff and breaking bones or pulling muscles. When you have more stuff than you can manage or properly care for, the excess stuff attracts more dust, bugs, mold and germs – and for some, that can cause even more stress and a whole new set of health concerns.

Clutter slows you down

Clutter makes it hard to find what you need, *when you need it*. As a result, you end up wasting time and energy searching for things. You miss important deadlines because you have to re-do work or projects that you've already completed but can't find.

The visual distractions and constant chatter that clutter creates make it very difficult to stay on task. Because of that, we tend to go around in circles, never really accomplishing anything from start to finish. Our days are spent frantically trying to "put out fires."

Clutter robs you of time, money and energy

Cluttered surroundings drain us of more time and energy than we realize. Stuff takes a lot of time and energy to manage. The more stuff you have, the more time it takes to manage it. Not only does it take a lot of time just to manage our stuff, we waste time searching for things we know we have but can't find!

We lose a lot of money paying late charges on bills we misplace, buying things that we already have but can't find and replacing things that were broken because they got lost in the clutter. When the greater portion of your kitchen is literally under the pile, you spend money eating out because there is no room to cook. Not to mention that a portion of your house payment or rent and utilities is being wasted on using that space to store a bunch of stuff that doesn't enrich your life — rather than being able to use that space to *live in*. In many cases, people even pay a monthly fee for additional storage units so they don't have to part with their stuff.

Being in a cluttered room is a big mental drain and leaves you feeling hopeless, exhausted and buried. Our clutter begins to dictate how we spend our free time. Rather than hanging out with family and friends doing things we love to do, our time is spent managing our overabundance of stuff.

Clutter sabotages your relationships

People whose homes have been overtaken by clutter are normally too embarrassed to invite friends or family over even though they want to. Relationships suffer because of the conflicts that come with clutter. Spouses and family members argue about the clutter and excess. Kids resent their parents for the missed social opportunities when their field trip slips aren't turned in or party invitations are lost.

Clutter derails you from your destiny

Here's the biggie in my opinion: **Clutter and disorganization stop people from going after their lives with gusto and enthusiasm.** Since managing clutter consumes so much time and energy and distracts us from the here and now, our goals and dreams are endlessly put on hold. When our spaces are full of things that are no longer useful, that leaves no room for good stuff to come in that would support our dreams or our lives now. We can't focus on our future and pursuing our goals because we are constantly distracted by our stuff.

Surrounding ourselves with a lot of clutter, endless activities and draining relationships, we unconsciously keep ourselves so busy that we're distracted from noticing and pursuing all that life has for us. Clutter keeps us from going after what we really want in life (because that can be a scary thing!). It also allows us to avoid bigger issues we may be trying to ignore, like the fact that we are keeping excess weight on to try to reduce the chance of meeting a significant someone who might hurt us one day. Hiding behind your clutter keeps the attention away from you and focused more on the stuff you have.

We've only skimmed the surface of the negative consequences of clutter. We'll take a deeper look at each type of clutter and the resulting impact it has on our lives in the following chapters.

It's your turn...

FOOD FOR THOUGHT:

If someone gave you a gift that you have no intention of ever using, and it is cluttering up your life, is there really a reason to keep it? Would the person who gave you that gift ever ask you to prove you still had it? What if you knew there was someone out there who *really needed* that item? Would it still make sense to keep it?

ACTION STEP:

1. Let's tackle your children's toys.
2. Skim the surface of the toys with your initial focus being to remove any broken toys.
3. Take another look back through the toys and pull out any of the toys that are seldom or never played with.
4. On your third pass, remove the ones that you know the kids never liked, but you held on to them simply because they were a gift.
5. On your final pass, eliminate anything they have outgrown, any duplicates and anything with missing pieces.

RULES FOR SUCCESS:

1. For best results, tackle your children's spaces when they are NOT around. Be sure to remove all of the items that are going before your children return to the space, or they will pull things back out that you're letting go of.

Chapter 9:
The Impact of *Physical Clutter*

"The price of anything is the amount
of life you exchange for it."

– Henry David Thoreau, Author and Poet

It is a fact that no two physical objects can occupy the same space at the same time. Knowing that, we must understand that when we choose to keep something, we are giving up the option of keeping something else in that space. When you have physical objects around that you no longer need, use or love (or things that don't support your life or current goals), there is no space left for the things that do support your life and goals to come in. We'll take a look at just a few of the endless ways that *physical clutter* negatively impacts your life in this chapter.

Clutter lies and tells you that you'll never succeed!

As mentioned in Chapter 8, clutter is constantly talking to you. It never shuts up! It reminds you of all of the things you forgot to do, all of the things you screwed up, all of the times you were hurt and all of the times you lost someone you loved. It reminds you of when you were thinner, younger or better in whatever way. This constant negative chatter repeatedly telling you all of the times you messed up serves as a continual reminder that you don't deserve to be successful.

The toys that are lying on the floor are demanding that you take action by screaming *"Hey, you unfit mother, I belong upstairs with the other Lego® blocks!"* The shoes that you have to return to the store because they are too small are yelling, *"You're such a loser. If you would have just taken the time to try me on before you bought me, then you wouldn't have to waste time taking me back to exchange me for another size!"* And the economy-size package of toilet paper sitting right inside the front door is saying, *"Really? Are you so lazy that you can't even take me to where I belong?"*

Clutter is rude. It is never your friend. It constantly lies to you by elaborating and embellishing every cluttered situation. Rather than saying your house is messy, it lies and insists that it is messy because you are a loser, worthless and can't do anything right. It always follows up the string of lies by telling you that you'll never be successful in anything you do because you're so stupid, lazy, etc.

Let's talk about the jeans you wore when you were three sizes smaller that you're holding onto because you hope to be able to fit back into them *someday*. The reality is that keeping them isn't moving you closer to your weight-loss goal. In fact, holding on to them is moving you further away because the jeans are constantly reminding you of your **failure** to stay in shape. They are screaming at you and calling you *"fatso"* all of the time. They are ridiculing you for even thinking you could fit back into them someday. This constant chatter beats you down, zaps your motivation and keeps you stuck.

A few years ago, I quickly gained a bunch of weight. Unfortunately it was right after I had finally gone out and bought new clothes. Because I detest shopping, I had put it off as long as I could. Sometimes I even put it off for years! I couldn't face the thought of going out and shopping again because my clothes no longer fit! However, after looking through my closet for something to wear and finding nothing day after day for months, I broke down and bagged up all of the brand-new clothes that no longer fit me. I easily and quickly filled seven trash bags and headed to my local Goodwill store. I grumbled the entire way there because now I wouldn't be able to deny that I didn't really have any clothes that fit me, and I would have no choice but to shop for ones that would fit.

After dropping off the clothes, I felt a new sense of freedom. It was then that I realized that as I had looked through my closet for something to wear each day, my clothes had been calling me "fatty" – each and every day! They reminded me daily of how much I had let myself down by gaining the weight. And on top of that, I realized I had been wasting precious time fruitlessly looking for something to wear in a closet full of things that no longer fit! Now I could easily see what clothes I had (which wasn't much!), and I wasn't reminded daily of my personal failure every time I perused my closet.

Without even realizing it initially, after letting go of the jeans and other clothes that were too small for me, I almost immediately felt more motivated and empowered to lose the excess weight I had gained because I didn't have that daily reminder of my failure that kept me beaten down and immobile. I successfully lost 35 pounds in the four to six months following this one action of removing the clothes that I could no longer use (a.k.a. clutter).

When you keep unnecessary stuff, it is always screaming at you and reminding you of things you would be better off forgetting. And remember, it is always telling you crushing and exaggerated lies.

Clutter steals your todays

When your home or office is full of material things from your past, you can't focus on the task at hand, much less your future or pursuing your dreams because you are constantly distracted by the memories of the past those items trigger. The items and associated feelings interrupt our current thoughts whenever we see them.

It would be completely absurd and preposterous to suggest that you shouldn't hold on to anything from your past. Once again, the key here is excess. As with anything, it's important to set boundaries and limits when it comes to how much stuff you'll keep from your past. Most of the memorabilia from your past (trophies, baby clothes, awards, etc.) is better left stored out of sight in the basement, except for a few chosen trinkets that you display in your living space.

When it comes to deciding whether or not to keep something from your past, one of the often overlooked steps is slowing down long enough to allow yourself to explore the feelings associated with each item. Just because it belonged to someone you loved or was a gift from someone you loved, doesn't mean you should hold on to it. If that relationship ended badly, many times there are negative feelings associated with those items. Although you may have loved the item when you were in that relationship, the item no longer triggers those same happy feelings it once did. Instead, it triggers the memories of that painful breakup. Of equal importance, when you are surrounded by stuff from your past, the memories jump out at you when you least expect them.

We are often called in to work with adult children who are left to deal with their parents' stuff after they have passed away or suddenly been moved from their lifelong home because of illness. As you can imagine, this task would be overwhelming in any case, but dealing with it at a time of loss, or when your parents need your love and support to help them through the transition, makes it ten times more stressful and difficult to do alone.

Many times the adult children will simply move everything from their parents' home to their home or a storage unit, thinking they will deal with it all later. What they don't realize is that by not dealing with it and simply moving it into their space, they are impacted by each and every item every time they come into contact with it. You would assume that anything associated with your parents would bring happy memories, but that is definitely not the case.

Their material belongings can trigger feelings of anger because you are left with the responsibility of dealing with all of their stuff that they didn't deal with. It can trigger feelings of sadness if the item represents the illness that took their life or caused them to have to move into an assisted living facility.

Their unfinished projects make you feel pain because you realize they won't ever finish them. The thought of letting go of any of their beloved stuff triggers great feelings of guilt and so on. Having these negative feelings jump out at you at the most inopportune times can play havoc when you're trying to focus on the task at hand or your current goals.

CLUTTER TRUTH #17:

Clutter triggers an emotional response that is not always positive.

If you are mentally and emotionally not able to deal with a loved one's possessions immediately, box things up and store them in an out-of-the-way place to *quiet the chatter* until you're ready to deal with the stuff and emotions that it triggers.

Clutter stresses you out!

The constant lies and negative chatter of your clutter reminding you of all of the things you haven't done, or all of the things you used to do so much better, puts an enormous amount of pressure on you and increases your stress level significantly. *Since clutter never stops talking, if you are surrounded by it, there isn't a peaceful place to regroup, refresh or relax.*

Not being able to find the things you need, *when you need them*, can send your stress level through the roof! Being surrounded by clutter increases your chances of having this situation occur on a regular basis, thereby increasing your stress level on a regular basis as well.

Physical clutter has the same effect on your brain as multitasking does because all of your stuff is clamoring for your attention at the same time – constantly. It overloads your senses, fogs your focus and increases your stress.

There's nothing that I find more peaceful than walking along my favorite creek. I go there when I need a mental break to escape the pressure and stress of everyday life. The calming sound of the water as it peacefully flows past is serene and refreshing. I am mesmerized watching the little waves and ripples that the water makes as it seamlessly glides over the rocks. The warmth of the sun relaxes my body as it shines down on the creek; my reflection bounces back to me from the water's surface.

The beauty and serenity the creek provides changes when fallen twigs and branches begin to clutter and pile up in it. Suddenly the water isn't flowing as effortlessly as it was before. The peaceful and tranquil sounds are replaced by splashing sounds as the water fights and struggles to move through the

59

pileup. The forceful flow of the water pushes additional sticks and logs into the clog. I no longer hear the calming sound of the water as it flows past me. Rather you hear the loud whoosh of the water flow stopping as it hits the pile of debris that is clogging up its natural flowing rhythm.

Our lives can look and feel like this when we don't deal with our clutter.

Clutter robs you blind!

Very few of us realize just how much clutter costs us or how much we're paying just to house or store our excess stuff. When you think about the various places in your home or office that clutter has rendered unusable, you must realize that a portion of your house payment and utilities is going toward the space that you can no longer use to live or work

60

in. If you're paying for a storage unit (or two or three!), that expense can quickly add up.

CLUTTER TRUTH #18:

Weigh the cost of losing the prime real estate to store the things you rarely, if ever, need or use.

If your desk drawers are full of books you never look at, is it worth giving up that space when the result is that you have to walk across your office every time you need an envelope or pen?

When you have to park your car in the driveway or on the street because the garage is too full of other things, you are not only exposing your car to the elements (hail damage, fallen branches, etc.), but you are also putting your car at risk of being broken into or stolen. All of these consequences have a financial impact.

With clutter, a significant amount of money is unnecessarily spent buying things because you can't find the ones you already have, or you didn't even realize you already had them. You spend money replacing things that are broken in the piles of clutter. Tossing expired foods that were lost and overlooked in the back of the cabinet, pantry or refrigerator takes a hit on our pocketbook as well.

There are medical expenses as a result of falling or tripping over your clutter. The increased dust, mold and germs that are often associated with excess stuff increase your risk of illness and the medical expenses that go along with them. Sometimes those expenses are accompanied by a loss of income during your time spent off work recovering.

Bills are easily lost and forgotten amidst the clutter. There is a variety of financial implications as a result of not paying your bills, or paying them late. Companies charge late fees, service charges and reconnection fees if your utilities are turned off. You could have additional expenses as a result of the utilities being turned off, like pipes that freeze and burst, or spoiled food. When you miss a credit card payment, or pay it late, it affects your credit and many times can result in an increase in the interest rate you pay for using your credit cards.

A cluttered environment definitely has a negative financial impact. In my work as a certified professional organizer, it is not uncommon to find checks that have not been cashed, gift cards that have not been used or money overlooked in greeting cards because they got lost in the clutter and people forgot they had them.

Not only that, we find information and paperwork that has gone untouched that notifies people they are entitled to refunds, bills that have gone unnoticed that indicate they were overcharged or charged more than once for the same thing and so on. As I frequently say, it truly does "pay" to get organized.

Through my work with clients, I have learned that mail and paperwork are an extreme problem for a great majority of people. Eighty-five-year-old Jack, his 86-year-old brother James and their 89-year-old sister Nancy knew this struggle all too well. Since the three siblings never married or had children, they lived together their entire life!

Without many other financial obligations, the three of them had a lifelong practice of giving money to charities to help the needy. What they didn't realize was that charities have a common practice of sharing donor contact information with other charities. It spreads like wildfire. Before long, their mailbox was brimming over with junk mail on a daily basis.

As they began to age, the struggle to maintain order in their home became more and more difficult. With James and Nancy beginning to show increased signs of dementia and no children or family to help them keep things under control, Jack had his hands full just caring for his two aging siblings.

An overabundance of mail, medical supplies and other things continued to come into their home on a regular basis, eventually leaving them with just narrow pathways to walk through in most of their home. When emergency workers responded to a call after Nancy fell while trying to retrieve the newspaper, the siblings were put on notice that they would be evicted from their home if things weren't cleaned up.

That's when we were called in to help. Believe it or not, we found close to $90,000 in cash and uncashed checks and bonds buried within the clutter of their home! Of course, this was an extreme case, but overall, we have found thousands and thousands of dollars in cash, uncashed checks and unused gift cards in many of our client's homes. With our ongoing help and home health care put in place, the siblings were able to remain in their lifelong home.

It's no doubt that most people are aware of *physical clutter* and the negative impact it has on our lives. In the next few chapters we'll examine some of the other types of clutter that people commonly struggle with.

CLUTTER TRUTH #19:
Junk mail multiplies quickly, especially when left unattended.

The minute your address (or email address, for that matter) is out there, it becomes fair game for marketers. It's a common practice for companies to share your information with similar companies. It's essential that you take time to contact them and ask to be removed from their mailing lists. Of equal importance, register with the following websites to opt out of larger, national mailing lists. (Imagine how many trees you'll save by removing yourself from these lists too!)

www.dmachoice.org
www.optoutprescreen.com

It's your turn...

FOOD FOR THOUGHT:

If your tendency is to save everything and/or you have trouble letting go of things, you must think about whether or not it is really worth all of the stress that comes with keeping it. Is it more valuable to you to keep it all, than to be able to walk in your house without tripping over things, being able to find what you need, being embarrassed to have company over and not being able to have any open space?

ACTION STEP:

If you're ready to take action to reduce the amount of mail (and email) that invades your home and computer, here's how you can get started:

1. Register with the two agencies mentioned in *Clutter Tip #19*.
2. Contact companies directly as you continue to receive mail from them after registering with the two agencies and request to be removed from their mailing list.
3. Unsubscribe from email lists rather than just deleting the unwanted email each time it comes.
4. Guard your contact information. It has become acceptable for stores, restaurants and others to request your email or home address for every purchase you make. When asked for this information, simply refuse to provide it. Keep in mind that information is not necessary to make the purchase, though they will try to make you think it is.
5. Quickly and easily opt out of receiving the white and yellow page directories at www.YellowPagesOptOut.com.

Chapter 10:
The Impact of *Time Clutter*

"The key is not to prioritize what's on your schedule, but to schedule your priorities."

– Stephen Covey, Author and Speaker

In Chapter 3 we learned that *time clutter* is when your time is spent doing things that don't bring you any closer to your goals or to the things that matter most to you in your life. It's when you fill your time with things you don't need to do or don't want to do. Your schedule and days are packed full of things to do that don't bring any value to your life or serve your greater good.

Time clutter is also when you have more appointments scheduled than the amount of time you have available for those appointments. When you schedule more commitments than you have available time, you cut into the time that you could be spending focused on the things that you really *do* enjoy and that matter most to you in your life, as well as those things that bring you closer to your goals.

Time clutter plays havoc with your health

Cramming meetings, appointments and other things into every nook and cranny of our time is the perfect recipe for disaster. Having more appointments than available time leaves you in a constant state of stress and anxiety. Running from one thing to the next doesn't allow adequate time to prepare for your next meeting or appointment (or recover from your last one!), which also increases your stress level.

Since you overschedule your time, you spend the majority of your days stressed and distracted because you are so worried about making it to the next meeting or appointment on time. Because of that, you struggle to be present at your current meeting or event, and can't give it the time or energy that it deserves or requires. This not only makes your meetings less productive, it also plays havoc with your health.

It's difficult to pin down an efficient step-by-step plan to reach your goals when you are not 100% invested in the task at hand. *Time clutter* weighs on you constantly and drains you mentally and physically.

Time clutter impacts your productivity and bottom line

Spending your time focused on the wrong things has monetary consequences. When your days are spent putting out fires rather than proactively working in your business, it negatively impacts your productivity. If you continually squeeze unnecessary or low priority things into your schedule – you're never going to get ahead of the game. Many of us have a hard time saying no. Something you may not have realized though is that when you say yes to everything, you are unknowingly saying no to the things that really do matter because you've now *given up* the time you would have spent on that to spend it doing something you would have been better of just saying no to in the first place.

As a successful young attorney whose business really took off before she had a chance to set up systems so that things would run smoothly, Karen was at her wit's end before she picked up the phone to call me for help. She said her main challenges were time management and paperwork. She felt like she was working 24-hours a day and still not seeing any light at the end of the tunnel.

Because she didn't have any order in her office, she spent all of her time putting out fires rather than taking care of things properly and efficiently. As a result of not having a system set up to track her billable hours with clients, she frequently neglected to mark down the time she spent on the phone with her clients or working on their cases. On the rare occasions that she would remember to jot it down, the scrap of paper she used would get lost and buried under the piles of paperwork on her desk rather than getting documented on her client's invoice. Needless to say, she lost a lot of income this way!

Karen also had a big, caring heart. She would continue to work with clients even when they weren't paying her. Since she didn't have a system for billing or following up on payments, she never took the time to really figure out how much her big heart was costing her. Not only was she working with people and not charging them, she was investing so much time and energy into these undesirable clients that she was seldom able to give as much time and energy to her paying clients as she should.

Regretfully, Karen began seeing how much her time clutter was impacting her bottom line once we started working together. After sorting through all of the paperwork in her office, we ended up with seven file boxes full of client files that were never paid. These boxes didn't include the clients that were never even billed for her time! One box alone added up to $29,000 she had lost in income. Multiply that by the seven boxes and you get a loss of $203,000!

Working together, we set up systems to avoid this in the future. First and foremost, the exercise of going through the files and seeing exactly what the time clutter was costing her helped her to be stronger in the future when it came to squeezing too many things into her schedule. She was also able to see that if she discontinued working with the clients that were taking advantage of her, she wouldn't be working nearly as hard and could focus more of her time, energy and expertise on the clients that did pay and appreciate her.

We began by creating a client tracking system that worked for her. The client tracking sheet lived right under her phone so it was a constant reminder to her each time she picked up the phone that she needed to mark down those types of calls. The client tracking sheet was given to her assistant to enter into their billing system weekly. We hired an outside company to handle all of the billing, including sending out monthly invoices. Together we created rules and systems for dealing with the people that weren't paying their invoices in a timely manner. We decided when her clients would be given warning letters if their bills weren't paid and when their attorney/client relationship would be terminated if they didn't pay. Once those rules were established, we delegated that responsibility to the outside billing company.

Though she had to invest time she didn't have to work with me, the investment paid off a million times over. By creating systems that proactively focused on keeping time clutter out of her schedule, she was better able to focus on her work and keep better track of billing her clients. Because she no longer felt like she had to work 24 hours a day, she was able to get to the gym more, hang out with friends and have downtime to rejuvenate.

CLUTTER TRUTH #21:

Take a realistic look at how *you want* to spend your time and schedule things accordingly.

Rather than just scheduling your life away with appointments and commitments, take some time to think about how you would *ideally* like to spend your time. Once you know what *your priorities* are and how much time you'll need to accomplish them, block out that time and schedule everything else *around* them.

Time clutter makes a mess out of your social life!

People who struggle with *time clutter* often make promises to attend events, only to end up letting people down by being late or not showing up at all because they are overcommitted. Relationships suffer as a result of these broken promises, conflicts and disappointments.

Time clutter limits your greatness!

When we overschedule our lives with tasks, errands, volunteering, working overtime, favors for others and our own to-do's, we are left with little time to create a meaningful life. We go from the cradle to the grave simply being busy rather than participating in all of the wonderful things life has for us!

Figuring out who we are and what makes us tick requires quiet reflection time. We can't focus on our future and pursuing our dreams when we are constantly consumed by an overwhelming abundance of activities and commitments.

Time clutter is such an easy thing to fall victim to. Just becoming aware of your scheduling habits can help you begin to make changes in this area that will simplify your life and allow you to focus on what's important. We'll take a closer look at *mental clutter* in the next chapter.

It's your turn...

FOOD FOR THOUGHT:

"Lack of direction, not lack of time, is the problem. We all have 24-hour days." – Zig Ziglar

ACTION STEP:

Here are five quick and easy habits to increase your productivity:

1. Group similar tasks together. When you make all of your phone calls back to back or pay bills all at once, it minimizes the amount of wasted time spent switching back and forth between projects.
2. Tackle the most difficult task on your to-do list first. After that the rest of the day should be smooth sailing!
3. Start each and every day (or do it the night before) by planning and prioritizing what you'll need to accomplish in order to use your time most efficiently.
4. Block off time in your day to work with little or no distractions or interruptions. Silence your phone and close the door. Initially the thought of doing this will seem unrealistic if you've never considered this option before. But it is the best thing you can do to increase your effectiveness and productivity.
5. Do not check your email until you have had ample time to focus on *your* priorities for the day. Emails have a tendency to set your agenda for the day if you allow them to.

RULES FOR SUCCESS:

1. Notice your natural tendency to slide back into your old habits of letting others dictate how your day will be spent, and re-adjust your course as quickly as possible.

Chapter 11:
The Impact of *Mental Clutter*

"The reason people give up so fast is they
tend to look at how far they still have to go
instead of how far they've gotten."

– Unknown

As we explored in Chapter 4, *mental clutter* is when
your mind is filled with past hurts or regrets and
when you are busy trying to remember too many
things at once. Multitasking creates *mental clutter*
because it splits your mind between projects or
ideas. Just as with any type of clutter, *mental clutter*
has very negative consequences when left
unattended.

*Mental clutter isn't always negative thoughts.
Great ideas and plans can cloud our minds too
when there are too many of them. Remember,
clutter always has the excess component in it.*

Mental clutter robs you of clear thinking

Mental clutter robs you of clear and focused
thinking. When your mind is full of a variety of
thoughts, ideas and emotions that are competing
for your attention, it's hard to give 100% to what
you should be focused on. *Mental clutter* results in

your mind constantly trying to multitask since there are so many thoughts and ideas vying for your attention.

If you're still upset about what your coworker said an hour earlier, the other thoughts and feelings associated with that will fog up your mind and block your creativity. *Mental clutter* crowds out the things our brains should be focused on in the here and now.

Mental clutter attacks you in your sleep

Needless to say, when your mind is working overtime to keep up with a barrage of random thoughts, mental to-do lists and ideas that are demanding equal billing for your attention, your stress and worry increase dramatically!

Having a variety of things clamoring for your *immediate* attention puts a great degree of strain on you. Many times we don't even realize that it is the *mental clutter* that is making us feel so anxious. For many of us, we're even attacked at night when we're trying to fall asleep by all of the things chattering in our minds that we can't quiet.

Mental clutter clouds your decisions

Mental clutter is just like any other clutter in that it leaves us feeling exhausted and debilitated by the sheer volume of it. Unable to think clearly, we make poorly thought-out, quick decisions about things in an attempt to *quiet* the thoughts in our mind so that we feel like we've regained some type of control.

Each one of us has a natural dialogue within ourselves that we tend to believe by default because we've heard the same thing from it over and over throughout our lives. If your natural internal dialogue has been a negative one, this increases your urge to make quick decisions on things even if they aren't well thought out because you feel like you have to work harder and faster to be good enough.

Mental clutter steals your joy

When your mind is full of past (or current) hurts or traumatic situations, it makes it difficult to engage fully in life. We're unable to see the beauty and blessings right before our eyes because the thoughts from the past are covering up the here and now by competing for our attention.

If past issues aren't dealt with, those memories frequently creep back into our minds, often at the most inopportune times, causing us to miss the joy-filled moments right in front of us. When the traumatic experiences from our past are disregarded and neglected, we carry around guilt and shame that is better forgotten. These negative feelings and thoughts fill our minds and don't allow space for positive, reaffirming thoughts to enter.

Mental clutter leaves you feeling paralyzed

Mental clutter is when there are an excessive amount of thoughts, ideas, distractions and to-do's that are competing for your attention at any given time. The sheer volume of things demanding your immediate attention leaves you feeling unsure where to even start – so you don't.

This is where procrastination sneaks in. Since you feel that you don't have enough control to give each thought the proper attention it needs to make a rational decision, you simply choose to try to avoid it all together. *As we've already discussed though, you can never ignore clutter, no matter what type, because it never shuts up!*

The electronic age has only served to make this problem bigger. With smartphones and tablets in everybody's hands, or within arm's-reach, that are set to alert you each time the wind blows, distractions have gone through the roof. These alerts only add to the overwhelming, out-of-control feeling you have from the overabundance of things clamoring for your immediate attention and brain power.

Mental clutter jumbles up your thoughts

In order to be productive, we have to have plans and systems in place to efficiently handle our projects and tasks. When our minds are full of competing thoughts, it's hard to quiet our minds long enough to think through effective systems for processing our workload.

Without systems in place, most of the time, our focus and energy are spent on putting out fires rather than being proactive. If you're trying to juggle and retain everything you're supposed to do and remember along with all of the other *mental clutter,* you're fighting a losing battle.

It's crucial that you establish systems that allow you to capture the overabundance of information and tasks from your mind somewhere so that you can readily access it when and if it is needed. Doing this helps to free up your mind so that it can focus solely and efficiently on the task at hand, and it gives you the peace of mind knowing you have that important information elsewhere, in an accessible place.

CLUTTER TRUTH #23:

Create systems to record your thoughts and ideas so your brain doesn't have to store them.

Establish systems to track your thoughts, ideas, birthdays and appointments using a calendar, email system or project folder, to name a few.

We have to harness our thoughts in order to rid ourselves of *mental clutter* and take back control of our minds. Remember, you are the only one who can decide what fills your head and shapes your thoughts. And only you can clear the mental distractions so you can focus on what matters most to you.

It's your turn...

FOOD FOR THOUGHT:

Remember, if we crowd our brains — and lives — with hurt feelings, there's little room for anything positive. It's a *choice you're making* to continue to feel the hurt, rather than welcoming joy back into your life. – John M. Grohol

ACTION STEP:

Three tips that help quiet *mental clutter:*

1. Exercise helps to keep you grounded by reconnecting your five senses to the present moment.
2. Forgive yourself for whatever mistake(s) you're holding on to. Acknowledge that you did your best with the situation at the time and move on (let it go!). You can't do it over again, so don't waste another minute fretting over it because you can't change it.
3. Start a journal. Regular writing can give you a safe, cathartic release of the road blocks and detours that you're struggling with in your mind.

RULES FOR SUCCESS:

1. Make the mental decision to take control of your thoughts.

Chapter 12:
The Impact of *Relationship Clutter*

"You don't let go of bad relationships
because you stop caring about them.
You let go because you start caring
about yourself."

– Charles J. Orlando, Relationship Expert and Author

Healthy relationships are created with a give-and-take connection where both parties feel supported, accepted and understood. They share common interests that help them to connect and bond. Healthy relationships tend to foster opportunity for growth and enrichment, along with increased feelings of self-worth and acceptance. One of the strongest signs of a healthy relationship is that both people involved feel good about themselves.

Relationship clutter is when your time is spent with people that break you down, rather than build you up. They focus on what you can do for them, rather than what they can do for you. These people always say they'll be there for you, but then never are. They take, take, take and seldom give back anything in return.

With *relationship clutter*, please keep in mind that if you are in a relationship where you are the one *giving* everything and the other person isn't giving anything back – **but you feel a great deal of satisfaction or a sense of helping someone that makes you feel good** – please realize that these relationships ARE adding value to your life because you are getting something good out of them. These types of relationships are NOT considered *relationship clutter*.

Relationship clutter steals the time that could be spent in healthy relationships

We've all played the strong, supportive and nurturing role with someone who was hurting or struggling in our lives. We pour time, love and energy back into their spirits to encourage them and give them hope. In these situations, our focus is on the other person, and we don't expect anything in return. This describes the normal give and take with any relationship. When they are down, you're there for them. When you are down, they are there for you.

However, if you're involved in relationships where you feel like you are constantly pouring love and energy on the other person and never getting anything in return, you have to ask yourself what value that relationship adds to your life. If you're not enjoying the relationship or getting anything positive from the interaction, why are you investing your time and energy in it? Remember, if you're spending your time in relationships that don't add anything to your life, you're also relinquishing the possibility for that time to be used for something or someone that does add value to your life!

Relationship clutter tells you that you're unworthy

Unhealthy relationships can be very damaging to your sense of self-worth. Spending time in disappointing relationships where your needs are not met and your emotions seem to be on a rollercoaster ride whenever you interact with that person leads to a gradual but steady erosion of your sense of self-worth.

Relationship clutter steals your confidence

Relationships that simply take and offer nothing in return drain you mentally and emotionally. They drain you of energy, motivation and confidence. When your needs are ignored, anger and resentment build and can lead to higher blood pressure and/or depression.

Relationship clutter derails you from focusing on your goals

When we choose to spend our time and energy in negative, one-sided relationships, we forfeit using that same time and energy to create and foster positive relationships – or working toward our goals and the things that make us happy. Invariably, when you spend time in relationships that don't add any value to your life, the relationship ends up pulling you further away from your goals and what matters most in your life.

CLUTTER TRUTH #25:

Don't be afraid of some empty space.

So often people fill their homes with *physical clutter* to keep their minds busy so they don't have to face their current situation – which many times is simply that they are alone and lonely. With *relationship clutter* we're doing the same, filling our lives with unhealthy relationships just so we don't have to be alone. As with any clutter, it's amazing what wonderful things have space to come into your life once you remove the bad or unnecessary stuff that is taking up that space currently.

It's your turn...

FOOD FOR THOUGHT:

"A good relationship is when someone accepts
your past, supports your present and
encourages your future." – Unknown

ACTION STEP:

In the majority of your relationships, look for people
that:

1. Value you.
2. Respect you.
3. Are honest with you.
4. Are trustworthy.

RULES FOR SUCCESS:

1. Don't ignore the red flags.
2. Listen to your gut instinct about the
   relationship.

Chapter 13:
The Impact of *Visual Clutter*

"Until you remove the noise,
you're going to miss a lot of signals."

– Seth Godin, Author and Speaker

As a reminder, *visual clutter* is when there is an excessive amount of things crowded together in a chaotic order within your view that compete for your attention.

Visual clutter hijacks your thoughts

The distractions and constant chatter that the *visual clutter* creates makes it difficult to stay on task. It pulls your attention away from what your focus should be on and zaps your creativity. *Visual clutter* has the same impact that multitasking does.

When your mind is pulled in several different directions at the same time, it's unable to devote the necessary attention to complete the task at hand in an efficient manner. With the constant distraction of *visual clutter,* we tend to go from one thing to the next and seldom accomplish anything from start to finish.

Visual clutter increases your stress

Sitting at your desk trying to focus on processing your email can be a losing battle when you can see the various things on your desk that you still need to do. The unpaid bills, to-do lists, meeting notes and mail you need to open are pulling your focus away from your email. Your stress level increases when there is *visual clutter* in your view causing your attention to be pulled in several directions at once. Add to that the additional pressure you feel when you see other things you need to do but haven't done yet.

Visual clutter makes you feel as if you're under constant attack by the enemy. When your days are spent working overtime to battle against feeling defeated by that, it creates a continual unnecessary source of stress – which eventually causes you to just shut down. Taking time to clear the *visual clutter* will strongly impact your stress level and productivity in a positive way.

CLUTTER TRUTH #26:

Create systems that effectively reduce *visual clutter* but doesn't let things fall through the cracks.

Many of us, including myself, are visual people. We have to see our tasks in order to remember we have to do them. Rather than leaving everything lying out in an unorganized manner, create systems that will track your tasks and ensure their completion without creating *visual clutter*.

Visual clutter blurs your thought process

Having to battle opposing things competing for your attention on a regular basis wears you down and leaves you feeling frustrated and tense, which results in a fight-or-flight response. In our rush to clear away as much *visual clutter* as possible, we tend to make poor decisions and choices that are not well thought out.

It's your turn...

FOOD FOR THOUGHT:

The less clutter you have, the more the things you love will get the recognition they deserve.

ACTION STEP:

Another common breeding ground for *visual clutter* is on a refrigerator. If your fridge is covered with papers, pictures and magnets, use these tips to clear the unnecessary stuff.

1. Look at each item individually by removing them one by one and holding them in your hand.
2. Ask yourself if you still need the information on the magnet or paperwork. If not, discard them.
3. Ask yourself if the pictures or items still hold the same meaning to you as they did when you first placed them there. If not, remove them.
4. If you have an overabundance of refrigerator magnets because "they're handy" – ask yourself how many you really need. Let go of the rest.
5. If you find there are a variety of addresses or phone numbers that you want to hold on to, create a master sheet to capture all of that information in one place. Be sure to include some extra blank lines to the master sheet so you can continue to add to the list.
6. Create rules for how long you'll display your children's artwork.

RULES FOR SUCCESS:

1. Think twice before just sticking something up on the refrigerator. Is there an alternate place you can keep the item?
2. Revisit the things on display frequently to avoid having them become a part of the kitchen scenery you no longer notice.

Chapter 14:
The Impact of *Food Clutter*

"In order to change we must be sick and tired of being sick and tired."

– Fannie Lou Hamer, Civil Rights Leader
and Philanthropist

As described in Chapter 7, *food clutter* is when your diet is filled with an *excessive amount* of food or drink that doesn't provide a valuable source of nourishment for your body. It's also when you consume more food than your body can use or process.

Food clutter causes weight gain

Stating the obvious, when you consume more food than is necessary to nourish your body, the impending result is weight gain. If you eat more food than you can burn off, you'll gain weight. Our bodies take what they need and then fill up the fat cells with the rest.

Food clutter results in poor self-esteem

We don't feel our best physically when we're overweight, and that shines through in the way we feel about ourselves. Consuming too much of anything makes us feel full and bloated. Those feelings also impact our self-esteem. Some foods even impact our mood, which can then affect our feelings of self-worth. For instance, sugar can lead to fluctuations in your blood sugar, which then brings on mood swings.

Food clutter reduces mental clarity

Research suggests that what we eat has a significant impact on how we think. When we consume things that don't nourish our bodies, it can create mayhem with our mental clarity. Some foods spike our blood sugar while others cause it to plummet quickly. Carbohydrate-heavy meals and turkey cause drowsiness.

CLUTTER TRUTH #27:
Fill your diet with healthy foods.

If your diet is filled with healthy foods that help your body work better and keep you satisfied longer, you wouldn't feel the need to feed your hunger with things that don't nourish your body as often.

Food clutter increases health issues

Consuming more food and drinks than we need to nourish our bodies can lead to health issues like high blood pressure and obesity. The most common health problems when people consume too much food, or the wrong types of food, are diabetes, heart disease and strokes. Other health issues include sleep apnea, high cholesterol and respiratory problems.

Food clutter impacts your pocketbook

We all love a good deal, don't we? Who can pass up a "buy one, get one free" deal? Not many of us. But when you over-purchase things that you don't need, they simply end up clogging up your food storage space. When you have more food than you need, items can get hidden and lost behind other things causing the food to expire before you get a chance to eat it.

Now that we've explored the different types of clutter and the impact they have on our lives, we'll jump into some of the psychological reasons why we hold on to clutter in the next chapters.

It's your turn...

FOOD FOR THOUGHT:

"A healthy outside starts from the inside."
– Robert Urich

ACTION STEP:

If you'd like to rid your diet of foods that aren't nourishing your body:

1. Start slowly by *adding* healthy foods into your diet rather than focusing on the things you need to *subtract.*
2. Replace a sugary beverage with water.
3. Become highly aware of everything that you eat and why. For instance, if your child left four uneaten crackers on their lunch plate, I bet your tendency might be to eat those rather than wasting them. Instead, stop yourself and either put the crackers back in the box or out for the birds to eat.

RULES FOR SUCCESS:

With any lifestyle change, it's important to mentally prepare before beginning so that you have the tools and awareness you need to see it through. In order to successfully change anything, you have to take the time to notice the consequences of your current habits or behavior so that your motivation won't waiver.

Chapter 15:
Why Am I Holding on to This?

*"When every possession is special,
none of them are."*

– Kathi Lipp, Author

Now that you we've taken some time to learn about the various forms of clutter and how it can negatively impact our lives, we'll explore the many deep-rooted psychological reasons we hold on to it. Granted, my area of expertise is in professional organizing, not psychology – so I speak from experience only, not from any type of formal education on the matter.

However, through my experience working with hundreds of clients and talking with them about their relationship with their stuff and why they are holding on to it, I've witnessed the same psychological reasoning for holding on to things over and over again. I think as you read on you'll easily be able to identify yourself in some of the following chapters.

Delayed Decisions
We've already learned that clutter is anything that you don't need, use or love. And it's anything that doesn't move you toward your goals. If we know

that is our guideline for determining what clutter is, how do we still end up with so much of it? In short, **all clutter represents delayed decisions**. It's hard to believe that it's really just that simple, but it is.

Stuff of all shapes and sizes comes into our home, office and lives without much effort on our part. It takes both mental and physical energy to get it back out. Rather than taking the time to decide whether something brings value to our life, the great majority of us take the easy way out: We try to ignore the stuff so we don't have to expend the mental or physical energy of making decisions about whether or not we should keep something.

CLUTTER TRUTH #28:

Though getting organized appears to be an external thing, it truly signifies an internal change or shift in the way you view your stuff and its significance.

Fear

Many times we delay making decisions about things in our lives because we're afraid of the resulting consequence if we decide to let go of something. You're afraid the minute you give up that book you'll wish you had it again. You're afraid that as soon as you shred your bank statements (that is, if you still get them in the mail) that you'll need them for some reason and so on.

We're afraid if we decide to return or exchange a gift someone got us that they'll be mad at us for not keeping what they originally gave us, or that we'll hurt their feelings. The most frequently used fear-based response I hear for keeping something that is no longer needed is that **you might need it someday.** I bet you've thought that a time or two yourself.

Guilt

People hold on to unnecessary things to avoid the guilt that comes along with letting go of them. We hold on to our parents' stuff after they pass away because we feel guilty about parting with things that we assume must have been important to them.

We hang on to gifts that we don't like and know we'll never use to avoid feeling guilty about hurting the feelings of the person who gave us the gift. We hold on to things because we feel guilty that we bought something we really couldn't use after all and we don't want to toss it if there is nothing wrong with it.

Sort things into categories of like with like before making decisions on your stuff.

It's important that you take the time to sort any space you're decluttering and organizing into piles of similar stuff. For instance, medicine, bandages, bath soap and toothpaste would all go in a bathroom pile together. Paper, pencils, rulers and scissors would all go in a school or office supply pile together. Sorting things before you make decisions helps you to make better informed decisions because you can see how much of any given thing you have at a glance – rather than making decisions on each one individually where your tendency would be to keep it.

Emotions

There are so many emotions and feelings connected with our stuff – and not all of them are positive. We tend to hold on to unnecessary items because we want to avoid feeling the painful or sad emotions connected with them. The mere thought of trying to decide whether or not to hold on to something that has a strong memory attached to it stirs up anxiety and emotions that are sometimes just too big for us to deal with. To avoid reliving those emotions, we default to just keeping the items.

Denial

We hold on to stuff that represents a time in our life that we're not ready to let go of. We cling tightly to things that represent people in our lives that we've lost and aren't ready to say goodbye to. Holding on to stuff that represents those people and cherished times allows us to put off dealing with the emotions connected to the realities at hand.

The same is true when we hold on to clothes we can no longer wear because we've gained weight. A part of us wants to deny the reality that we may never be able to wear those cute clothes again. We hold on to things from our children's early days as a reminder not only of their youth, but of our own youth as well. The items remind us of a time when we knew exactly what our role or purpose was in life; by preserving the memories of yesterday's role, we don't have to admit that we're not quite sure what our role or purpose is today.

"I'm Gonna"™

My all-time favorite excuse for holding on to things that no longer have a purpose in someone's life, and the one I hear most often, is what I lovingly refer to as the *"I'm gonna"* excuse. The list of things that we're *"gonna"* do is endless.

"*I'm gonna*" fix it. "*I'm gonna*" give it to a friend. "*I'm gonna*" make something really cool out of it. "*I'm gonna*" return it to the store, and so on. I hope that after you've read this book that you will catch yourself every time you say "*I'm gonna,*" and then you will take a few more minutes to think through if you are really ever "*gonna*" do what you say you're going to do or not. More often than not, we don't do what we think we're "*gonna*" do.

Now that we've taken a quick peek at some of the psychological reasons we hold on to things that no longer serve a purpose in our lives, we'll dive into each one of them a little deeper in the following chapters.

It's your turn...

FOOD FOR THOUGHT:

If you hold on to the beautiful dish sets your late mother collected, but they are packed away in the basement – are they really honoring her memory? Wouldn't it make more sense to save only one of the pieces and display it? A boxed up set of dishes in the basement isn't doing anything to further her memory.

ACTION STEP:

1. Locate at least five things in the room you are sitting in that you *know* can go, but that you have just been holding on to rather than taking action to release them.
2. Off the top of your head, can you find 1-2 things that were gifts and you know you've only held on to them because they were gifts, not because you were ever going to use them? Today is the day to let those go.
3. Are there any potential projects that you've had lying around that you know you'll never *really* get to? Let's set those free today as well.

RULES FOR SUCCESS:

1. Decisions not followed with action don't change anything. Be sure to get things out of your home or office as soon as you make the decision that they can go. Don't put off taking those items away.

Chapter 16:
Delayed Decisions

"Clutter is the physical manifestation of unmade decisions fueled by procrastination."

– Christina Scalise, Author

Did you know that all clutter, whether it's the stuff in your home, the paper piles sitting on your desk at the office, or the *time clutter* that's filling up your calendar, is caused by the same thing? **All clutter represents delayed decisions**. It's hard to believe that it's really just that simple, but it is. **If you take only one thing from this book, this would be the thing I would hope you hold on to. It's the most important part of the solution when it comes to keeping clutter at bay.**

If it's that simple, then you may wonder why we don't just make the necessary decisions. We'll dig deeper into the psychology behind why it's so difficult to slow down and make these decisions in the next few chapters. However, the short answer is that we put off making these decisions because each item represents a multitude of questions we must ask, answer and act on. And each question seems to only bring more questions.

It's not as easy as just deciding whether you want to keep something or let it go. In order to decide if you want to keep something, you have to decide 1) why you need it, 2) what you'll use it for, 3) how often you'll use it, 4) where you'll store it and 5) what you'll store it in. If you decide to let go of something, you have to decide 1) where to take it, 2) how you'll get it there, 3) when you'll have time to get it there and so on. That's a lot of mental work for one item. The thought of doing that for every item in your home or office feels daunting and overwhelming. That's where professional organizers come into play; they help you break down the process.

As an example, let's think about a closet filled to the brim with shoes. You may start the questioning by simply asking yourself "Do I really need all of these shoes?" As you begin to answer that question, you are immediately bombarded by a barrage of other questions like "If I don't want them, what should I do with them?" Or, "What about all of the money I paid for them?" And then there's the good old standby "How can I get rid of them if they were a gift?" The questions come so hard and so fast that people become overwhelmed and just close the closet door. Hence, the clutter continues to grow until we find ourselves overpowered by it.

CLUTTER TRUTH #30:
Simplify the decision-making process by breaking it down.

Rather than trying to answer *every* question that comes to mind with each item you look at, initially keep your focus on just whether or not to keep the item. Be sure to set up clearly labeled boxes for KEEP, DONATE or TOSS to put your stuff in as you make those decisions.

Another reason we delay making the difficult decisions about our stuff is because the majority of us are auto-programmed to just keep everything. In this busy, fast-paced world we live in, it initially seems quicker and easier to just keep everything by default. It doesn't take any time, effort or energy on our part to just toss it out of sight somewhere in a drawer or closet or down in the basement. At least that's what we initially think. However, as we talked about in Chapter 2, it's not that simple. Keeping unnecessary things does impact your life in many negative ways. Clutter doesn't sit quietly anywhere for long. Eventually it grows and spreads, slowly creeping into your prime living spaces. Here's the catch: Even when you think you are not dealing with your clutter, the impending decisions are weighing on you mentally.

Unfortunately, stuff comes into our homes and offices at a rapid pace without much, if any, effort from us. Mail arrives daily. Stores and restaurants send you home with excess marketing paperwork and receipts. Friends and family send you home from visits with gifts and things they no longer want and are parting with. The kids drag things home from their friend's houses. The list goes on and on!

CLUTTER TRUTH #31:
Label items that need action taken.

As you work through and make decisions about your stuff, you will come across things that need to be returned or given to someone, that need to be repaired, that go in another room, etc. As you come across these items, label them with the action that is needed and gather them together in one area of the room until you can take action on them.

As we explore some of the other reasons we hold on to things in the following chapters, keep in mind that at the root of each of them is the fact that we are delaying making an informed decision about whether or not the item adds any value to our lives at all.

It's your turn...

FOOD FOR THOUGHT:

Imagine a tree that has been neglected for years and you're certain to picture one that looks very messy and unkempt, with branches going in the wrong direction, growing between other branches or that are hanging too low. This image can feel a lot like our cluttered home or office does.

Pruning a tree removes the dead, damaged and diseased branches in order to benefit the whole tree. Once pruned and properly cared for, trees immediately look like they have taken on a new life and a new direction. Finally free of the cluttered branches that weren't serving them, and that were actually harming them, they can now grow stronger and healthier.

The pruning process is a perfect example of our need to declutter, along with the positive after effect. Decluttering trims out the unnecessary stuff that is hindering our growth. It uncovers and opens up a new life and direction for us. Aren't you ready for that?

ACTION STEP:

1. Identify something that has a negative memory attached to it.
2. Ask yourself why you are holding on to it if it only triggers something bad.

RULES FOR SUCCESS:

1. If the only thing the item does is remind you of something bad, even if it belonged to someone you loved, it's time to let it go.

Chapter 17:
Fear

"It's okay to be scared. Being scared means you're about to do something really, really brave."

– Mandy Hale, Author

So many times our desire to avoid making decisions about the clutter in our lives stems from fear. We're afraid of the resulting consequences of making the decision. There is so much fear surrounding why we keep things that it's staggering.

Armed with this knowledge, it's important to take the time to slow down and acknowledge those fears as you make decisions about your stuff. Facing the fears head on is the best way to beat them. It's also very empowering!

"I might need it someday."

At the top of the list is the good old standby "I might need it someday." It's an easy excuse to automatically fall back on because you could say that about everything you own! "I might read that book again," "I might fit back into those jeans once I lose the extra weight," "I might finish that project," etc. We're afraid that as soon as we let go of something, we're going to need it. And then it will cost us money and/or aggravation to replace it. Or worse yet, we worry that we won't be able to repurchase that item again anywhere.

That is a fear-driven thought! Most people automatically default to keeping things out of the fear that they might one day use it or miss it if it's gone, rather than thinking that decision all of the way through. Just the fact that you haven't used it in the last one, two or three years generally means its once useful purpose has expired. If you keep it and need it in the future, will you even remember that you have it or where you stored it? Chances are greater that you will automatically jump in the car and head to the store instead.

In many cases, we incorrectly think that we won't be able to find that special item again. We believe that suddenly no one will ever make it. If you truly have something that is unique that you don't think you'll ever be able to replace, then maybe you should hold on to it. *Most of the time, the object we're afraid to let go of really isn't that extraordinary.*

The majority of the time we won't need the item we've let go of. Many times it's easier and cheaper to just go out and re-buy it if we find we need it later. With the money we've invested in managing it and storing it (house payment or rent and utilities for that space, and giving up the use of the space it took up), we've probably paid more for it than what it was actually worth just by holding on to it.

CLUTTER TRUTH #32:

Ask yourself what the absolute worst thing could happen if you let it go.

If you're holding on to something simply because you're afraid you might need it someday, ask yourself what is the absolute worst thing that could happen if you did let it go. If the cost of keeping it on hand outweighs the answer, let it go. It is especially important that you factor into your decision the volume of things you're keeping simply because you might need them someday.

"I'll forget them."

People are afraid to let go of the belongings of a loved one who has died, or someone who has moved away or abandoned them, because they fear that they may forget them over time. Holding on to an *excess amount* of their stuff doesn't keep their memory any fresher in our minds. Let's face it, generally as time passes, we do forget things about people no matter how many trinkets we hold on to.

If you do choose to keep a few of their things, be sure to choose only those things that make you happy or bring a smile to your face when you see them. Though you loved that person, some of their things can have a negative emotional response associated with them. When you keep those things as a reminder of that person, you're causing yourself to relive those painful feelings each time you see the item.

CLUTTER TRUTH #33:

Let go of items that trigger negative memories and emotions.

Just because an item belonged to someone you loved doesn't mean you should hold on to it. Not all of our loved one's belongings trigger happy memories or emotions. Let go of the stuff that conjures up negative feelings and memories.

If you're keeping things so you can remember someone better, those things should be displayed rather than packed up in a box somewhere. Otherwise, they really aren't serving the purpose you're keeping them for. For example, rather than keeping an entire unopened box (or two or three boxes!) of china in the basement for years and years, only to pass them on to your next of kin when you die, display a place setting to honor that memory and donate or sell the rest.

Hurt feelings

We hold on to a lot of things simply because we don't want to hurt someone else's feelings. It is true that many people put a lot of thought, time and energy into buying the perfect gift. Knowing that makes it difficult not to hold on to the item even when we don't like or need it, because we don't want to hurt the giver's feelings.

It is equally true, however, that many people rush out and grab whatever they see in order not to show up somewhere empty-handed. For most people, it is difficult to distinguish between the well-thought-out gift and the last-minute gift grab, so we assume that we must keep every gift we receive.

Once again, that is a fear-based thought and a boundary issue. People give gifts to those that they care about and want to do something special for. If the giver was aware their gifts were causing any type of anguish, they certainly wouldn't want that. Keep in mind that most people never come back and ask you to *prove* you held on to the gift they gave you. I realize there are people out there who get upset if you don't keep their gifts, and perhaps you should handle them with kid gloves. But for the most part, when it comes right down to it, it's your home, and you get to decide how much stuff comes into it.

Melissa and Sarah were great friends. They enjoyed hanging out over a cup of hot tea and chatting about anything and everything whenever they could. No topic was off-limits! The two friends shared so many things in common that there was seldom a lull in the conversation.

One thing they didn't have in common was their taste in clothes. Sarah would often send bags of clothes that she no longer wanted home with Melissa. We've all done that at some point, right? Although they wore the same size clothes, Melissa knew she would never wear the clothes her friend was giving her.

Since she didn't want to hurt Sarah's feelings, she would always politely thank her for the clothes and carry them home even though she KNEW she would never wear them. Eventually the untouched bags lined her hallway from one end to the other.

Since they were a gift, Melissa felt like she couldn't get rid of them. So there they sat...two rows of crumpled-up Dillard's bags lining her hallway, full of clothes she knew she would never wear. This pattern repeated itself over and over for years until Melissa finally decided that she had to risk hurting Sarah's feelings by telling her "no thanks" in the future. The solution was simple indeed, but it's *something we all commonly do to avoid hurting someone's feelings.*

Missing that one great piece of information

There are a lot of people out there who I lovingly refer to as *"information junkies."* They absolutely love information and learning. They can't get enough information – ever! They hold on to every magazine, book, article or email anyone has ever sent them. They are afraid that if they part with any of it, they will miss that *ONE* really great piece of information that they needed.

Although they really do want to read it all someday, and have every intention of doing so, they seldom have enough time to read it all. The amount of time they have available to read never matches the piles of reading they want to do. As a result, they default to holding on to all of the information in the hopes that they *will* get to read it someday. And at the very least, if they don't get to read it all, they assume they can refer back to it when needed.

However, by keeping all of the information, they'll never be able to find that one special piece of information they're looking for without going through everything they have. And realistically, they'll never search through it all. With today's technology, most of the information can be found online much quicker than it could be found in their piles.

Losing money

We hold on to things after their purpose in our lives has passed because we feel like we would be throwing away our hard-earned money if we let them go, especially if the cost of acquiring the item was significant. So instead, we keep things because we paid a lot of money for them even though they no longer provide any value to our lives. *But remember, you don't get your money back by keeping things!*

Many times we think we will sell items in an effort to recoup the money we paid for them, but the truth of the matter is that you cannot sell things for what you paid for them. In reality, you normally can only sell things for a pittance of what you actually paid for them. You are losing more money storing things that you don't need than you will ever make selling them.

With three teenagers at home and an exchange student visiting for three months, the Johnson family was quickly outgrowing their house and needed our help to get things back under control. The root of their problem stemmed mostly from the fact that although new stuff continuously came into the house, the family had not been diligent about getting things out that no longer served a purpose in their busy lives. Clutter had literally taken over their entire home, leaving most of the spaces barely useable or functional.

We started out by tackling their garage. To make more room in their small and cramped kitchen, we set up shelves in the garage to house the extra canned goods, paper towels, cleaning products, and larger dishes and party trays. While working with the husband and father, Jim, to make decisions about the value of everything in the garage and whether or not to keep things, we came across several pairs of shoes.

Once Jim decided which shoes he wanted to keep, I asked him to take the shoes that he said weren't used outside in the yard and put them in his closet. He agreed to do that with all of them except for one pair that he said he wanted to leave in the garage.

Since it didn't make any sense to keep other shoes in the garage that weren't used for working in the yard, I questioned him further to find out his reasoning behind this decision.

When I asked him why he would leave a pair of shoes out in the garage that he doesn't wear for yard work, he admitted, "Well. They are kind of tight." When I asked why he would keep a pair of shoes that were kind of tight, he said he had just bought them. When I asked him again why he would keep a pair of shoes that were too tight, he dodged the question. **Remember, all clutter represents delayed decisions.**

Since he dodged my question, and it's my job to help people make good decisions about their stuff, I tried another approach. I asked him if he was faced with the decision to choose between the tight pair of shoes and another pair of shoes on any given day, would he ever choose to wear the tight shoes over a different pair? He finally admitted to me (but really it was to himself) that he probably wouldn't choose the tight ones because they didn't fit. By going through this coaching exercise with me, he realized that the shoes weren't bringing any value to him at all and that he was only holding on to them because he paid a lot for them. Once I explained that he wasn't going to get his money back by holding on to them, he was ready to let go of them.

Consequences of making the decision

Once you finally start making decisions to let go of the things that are no longer helpful in your life, you open yourself up to the consequences of making those decisions. Keeping the clutter protects you from the resulting consequences.

The big fear is that you *will* hurt someone's feelings if they find out you didn't keep their gift. You *will* need it someday. You *will* wish you still had it and so on.

A little-known fact is that the good consequences of letting go far outnumber the fears and any negative consequences of holding on to excess stuff. With every bit of clutter that you purge from your life, you are slowly peeling back the things that have helped you hide (or blocked you) from your dreams, and from a fuller life. You're afraid of the hurts and challenges that come with pursuing your dreams or living a full life.

Overwhelmed or not knowing where to start

Many times we feel afraid of the decluttering task itself. It can look so big, chaotic and time-consuming that we have no idea where to even begin. We feel overloaded by all of the decisions we know we'll have to make. We may also realize that once we start making decisions, we'll feel exhausted just trying to figure out what to do with the stuff we do or don't need or want. If we're already bogged down with life or our circumstances, we certainly don't want to create any more work for ourselves.

If you're ready to start tackling your clutter but don't know where to start, I'd recommend hiring a professional organizer to help and support you through the process. Professional organizers know how to break down the process to make it easier – and even a little fun! You can find organizers in your area by visiting the National Association of Professional Organizers (NAPO) website at www.NAPO.net.

Fear and delayed decisions are at the root of the clutter problem; what are some other reasons we hold on to stuff long past its usefulness in our lives? We'll dive into some other reasons we hold on to things longer than we should in the following chapters.

It's your turn...

FOOD FOR THOUGHT:

"Being organized is not about being perfect; it's about customizing your whole world to work FOR you." – Nealey Stapleton

ACTION STEP:

Let's take a closer look at your files. Many of the things in our files are kept out of fear. They are things we *think* we are supposed to keep, rather than things we have really thought about and *know* that we should keep for a specific purpose.

One of the most common mistakes I see is people keeping a copy of their paid bills and writing the date they paid it and the check or confirmation number for their payment. The argument for keeping them is so they can prove that they paid their bill. As I explain frequently though, you would *never* be able to take your bill stub in with your writing on it as proof of payment. No company would ever accept that. Instead, you'd have to get a copy of your cancelled check or contact the bank to remedy the situation. Therefore, the reason for keeping the bill stubs is negated.

Using this example, take a peek back through your files and think through your reasoning for what you're keeping. Is there *really* a purpose for what you've kept? Is there a true benefit for keeping it? Can the information be found elsewhere?

RULES FOR SUCCESS:

1. Don't get overwhelmed and default to just keeping anything. Force yourself to think through the true value of each file of paperwork you're keeping.

Chapter 18:
Guilt

"Guilt is always hungry – don't let it consume you."

– Terri Guillemets, Quotation Anthologist

There are so many feelings of guilt associated with the things we have and why we are holding on to them that it is astonishing! Remember how we described clutter in Chapter 1? Part of the definition of clutter is that it is anything that you don't need, use or love.

Therefore, you should not hold on to things simply because you would feel guilty about parting with them. It's critical to your success and happiness that your home or office houses only those items that make you happy and support your current life or goals.

CLUTTER TRUTH #36:

Your home or office should only house those items that make you happy or support your current goals.

Clutter is anything that you don't need, use or love. It's also anything that doesn't move you closer to your current goals. If you don't need it, use it or love it – why do you have it?

"But it was a gift!"

As we discussed previously, people incorrectly think that they have to save *everything* that someone gives them, even if they don't like it. It seems ungrateful to the person who gave us the item if we don't keep it. We wonder what we will say if they ask us where it is. We feel guilty if we don't keep it because someone took the time and energy to get it for us.

I guarantee that the person who gave you the gift meant it as a blessing. If they knew it was only adding to your clutter or stress level, they would not hesitate to tell you to toss it or re-gift it to someone else who *would* enjoy it!

"My child made it."

Many parents feel guilty if they don't keep all of the wonderful things their children make. Somehow it feels to them as though they aren't being a good parent if they don't keep the stuff. Or, they feel like it would mean that they must not love their children if they don't keep it all. The funny thing is that many parents spend years keeping these little nuggets *for* their children, yet the children many times don't even want them when they grow up. The truth is that these things mean more to the parents than the children.

If you keep a special picture, paper or art project here and there throughout the years, they hold more meaning than when you keep tub after tub of the stuff. **When we keep everything, then nothing is special.** If you keep everything through the years, you are also missing out on an opportunity to teach your children about limits and boundaries with their stuff.

Someone special to you loved it

When someone passes away, the most common course of action is to round up family and close friends to go through the loved one's belongings and take anything that is special to them before the rest of the stuff is donated or tossed. Many times the people who end up with the stuff don't have space or a need for it.

But because the stuff originally belonged to someone very special to them, they feel guilty if they don't hold on to it. They feel that if they let go of the stuff it means that the original owner was not special to them and that they are "tossing away" their loved one. As a result of those feelings of guilt, they want to honor their loved one's stuff in an effort to honor them – and to hold on to them.

You may also feel that by letting go of their stuff it will signify that you never loved them or that you no longer love them. If you slow down long enough to really think about it and acknowledge that this is an inaccurate feeling, you will be able to let go of the stuff while still knowing how much you loved that person.

I have seen countless basements, rooms and entire homes that have been taken over with a deceased loved one's belongings – sometimes stuff from several people who are now deceased. Although the stuff is causing headaches and stress, the guilt connected with letting go of the stuff makes us feel compelled to keep it out of respect for those that we loved – and *their* love for this stuff.

Just because your Grandma loved china and had five sets when she died, doesn't mean that you have to keep all five sets. Many times these things are just boxed up somewhere, never even opened. Why keep them if you don't ever even look at them or enjoy them? Just because Grandma loved it doesn't mean you have to.

"But it's their picture!"

A new trend has emerged in this digital age – people often send cards that have pictures of themselves, their families or pets on them. These are great because we feel like it gives us a better glimpse into what's going on in their lives, how they've changed, etc.

On the downside, many times the card's recipient feels obligated to keep it out of guilt because it has pictures of their friends or families on them. We somehow feel that if we toss the card it symbolizes that we're tossing the people in the picture – as if to say they are trash and unimportant to us. Nothing could be farther from the truth! Making a decision about whether or not to keep a physical card as a memento of your relationship has nothing to do with the strength of your friendship or feelings for that person.

"Look how much work they put into it!"

Have you ever ended up with something in your possession that you knew someone had put a lot of work and effort into? Maybe it's a binder they put together for you that is filled with their favorite recipes. Perhaps it's an afghan that they spent hours and hours crocheting for you.

If you don't consider yourself a person who enjoys cooking, or if you are like me, a person who simply doesn't cook – what use would you have for a recipe binder? I'd bet probably little to none. But because you recognize that the person who gave you the item invested a lot of time and energy into creating it, you would feel guilty letting go of it. So instead, you keep it though you know you'll never use it or need it.

As a result, it will lie up in the hall closet for the next 50 years or so until you die. Then, it will be passed down to the next unsuspecting victim who will keep it for the next 50 years or so until they die, simply because they will assume that it must have been important to you. And so now, out of guilt, it's important to them.

"There's nothing wrong with it!"

This is another big one. We assume that we must keep everything, especially when there is nothing wrong with it. We feel guilty about letting go of things that are still working and in good condition, even if their purpose or value in our lives has passed. The guilt associated with knowing that someone else could probably use or repurpose the item causes us to hold on to it in the hopes of connecting it with the person that will cherish it – even though we know we'll never get around to making that connection.

The key to keeping clutter at bay is that the amount of stuff that is coming in has to equal the amount of stuff that is going back out. You will lose the clutter battle every time if you keep everything just because it works and is in good condition. Remember, only keep those things that you need, use and love. The rest is clutter – even if it's still in good condition!

CLUTTER TRUTH #37:

The amount of stuff that is coming in must equal the amount of stuff going back out.

It takes little or no effort from us for clutter to come into our lives, so we have to be ruthless about getting it out. The only way to keep clutter at bay is to proactively work to get unnecessary things out.

Are you beginning to see yourself and why you hold on to things in some of the examples and explanations in this book? My hope is that by becoming aware of your natural tendencies and reasoning for keeping unnecessary stuff, you will be empowered to change the way you look at your stuff. But what about our emotions? What role do they play in all of this?

It's your turn...

FOOD FOR THOUGHT:

"The most important things in life aren't things."
– Anthony J. D'Angelo

ACTION STEP:

The true art of keeping clutter at bay is being intentional about what you acquire. Life is so busy that many times we just dash out and buy things without thinking about it. The key here is to slow down and think it all of the way through before dragging an item home or to the office with us.

1. Notice your mood. If you're sad, bored, lonely or having other negative feelings, it is best to avoid shopping as a pick-me-up.
2. Watch out for "great deals" or bargain basement pricing that causes you to shift from focusing on what *you* need to what *they* are trying to sell you.
3. It's easy to want to do lots of things with our life, but we have to check in with our current reality before committing to those things. So rather than running out and buying a bunch of things to support our latest urge to start juicing, start exercising at home or whatever else your heart desires at the moment, take time to see if it's something you can realistically add to your plate before buying the new exercise machines, juicing supplies, etc.

RULES FOR SUCCESS:

1. Think about everything you acquire in great detail to ensure that you really do need the item and have a *true* purpose for it.

Chapter 19:
Emotions

"People don't buy for logical reasons.
They buy for emotional reasons."

– Zig Ziglar, Author and Speaker

Without even realizing it or questioning why, we automatically place great value on all of our stuff. Because of that, we have a protective tendency to cling tightly to it. What we don't realize is that it's usually not really the item that we want to keep, it's the memory that the item triggers or represents that we want to hold on to – or conversely, the negative memory that we want to avoid.

There are so many emotions wrapped up in our stuff, both good and bad. The anxiety and feelings of dealing with those items, and making decisions of whether or not to keep them, stir up emotions that are just too big for us to deal with. If we default to just keeping the items, then we don't have to feel the emotions that letting go of them would provoke.

"Wait! That was my Great Aunt Myrtle's!"

In Chapter 17 we touched on the fear-based reason we hold on to a deceased loved ones belongings –

the fear that we'll forget them. But that's not the only reason. When someone we love passes away and we're left with their stuff or something they gave us, we hold on to it whether we like it or not because we're not ready to deal with the emotions tied to letting go of it. If we let go of their stuff, then we are faced with feeling the pain and complete loss of that person again.

"This is the last piece I have from when I was married."

When we've gone through a tough divorce or breakup (is a divorce or breakup ever not tough?), we cling tightly to the things we have left over from that relationship because they represent a time when it was intact and life was still as it seemed it should be. We hold on to that because it's easier than dealing with the emotions that would come if we let go of it. Letting go of the stuff from our past marriage represents having to let go of the all-American dream of the perfect family life and the feelings of failure or betrayal that come along with a divorce or the loss of a significant person that comes with any breakup.

Sometimes, as was my case, we end up with very few things from our married life after a divorce. Because we fought hard for those items during the divorce (and throughout the difficult marriage), we feel like we're not about to let go of those things

131

because we did fight so hard for them. Many times the items don't even hold much monetary value and could easily be replaced. Yet, we want those *specific* items because of the emotional turmoil we had to endure to secure them.

CLUTTER TRUTH #38:

Limit the number of your children's papers and projects that you save.

It's difficult to part with things our children created. But saving too many things decreases the importance or value of each one. Time and time again, I've seen well-meaning parents who have saved a TON of stuff for their children from their childhood. In almost a decade in business, I have NEVER seen a child who cared about, or wanted, any of it. Take pictures of the excess items if you must and then let them go.

"Joey made that in kindergarten!"

We hold on to our children's school papers and the things they make while growing up because of the feelings we have about each of their accomplishments or hurdles they overcome in life. These art projects and school papers remind us of the love and pride we felt when little Suzie scribbled with a crayon for the first time, or when Johnny glued together his first two strips of paper to form a unique art project.

Once again, we feel that if we part with anything our children made, it means that we don't love them; aren't proud of them; or that we are bad, unsupportive parents. Nothing could be further from the truth!

"I used to really be somebody!"

As much as many of us don't want to admit it, we're never really happy with who we are or where we are in life until we look back on a particular time period; then we can see a person who had it more together than we realized at the time. Because we continue to feel insecure throughout our lives, our stuff reminds us that at one point in our lives *we really were somebody important and had it all together*. Keeping that stuff provides us with encouragement and hope that we can be somebody important again one day.

Bad emotions

Something I don't think most of us realize is that any of our stuff that is associated with a loss (divorce, death, our youth) also triggers bad or painful emotions every time we see it. As I mentioned before, clutter never shuts up! It talks constantly – and it's *NEVER* saying anything positive! Although the memories quickly flash through our minds when we see the stuff, the memories bring painful emotions with them as well.

Although the stuff from "when we really used to be somebody" encourages us, it also beats us down by saying "Look at you now! You USED TO really be something! You've *really* let yourself go." A smaller pair of pants that no longer fits would conjure up feelings of failure and regret. The serving platter we received as a wedding gift reminds us that we let ourselves and others down when the marriage failed.

As our children get older, the things they made while growing up remind us that they aren't the only ones getting older; *we* are too. They remind us of a time when our children really needed us, which in turn made us feel important and as if we had a purpose in life. We may not have felt like that since they grew up. Although you may love the freedom that having grown children as friends brings, these things from their youth still stir up some negative emotions.

That chair that *he* always sat in reminds us of a happier time rather than where we are now – widowed, alone, and feeling sad and betrayed that he left us.

By holding on to this stuff to avoid the feelings associated with letting go of it, we are in fact doing ourselves a disservice. When we hold on to the stuff that brings up bad emotions, we have to experience those bad emotions over and over again rather than pushing through the emotions involved in letting go ONE TIME. Many times people try to avoid re-experiencing these emotions with the items they want to keep by "storing" (I say hiding) them in the basement so they don't have to deal with those memories.

CLUTTER TRUTH #39:

Release the guilt of impulsive purchases.

Holding on to a vase you never liked simply because you paid a lot of money for it only serves as a negative reminder of how frustrated you are at yourself for wasting that money. Let it go!

Emotion is one of the most common reasons people hold on to things. Can you think of a few things you're holding on to because of an emotional attachment? I know I can.

It's your turn...

FOOD FOR THOUGHT:

Decluttering and getting organized is an ongoing journey, not a one-time event.

ACTION STEP:

Have you ever wondered where a fork belongs? I highly doubt that you have. The reason we don't wonder where it goes is because it almost always has a designated home – in the utensil tray. Being organized means having a designated home for everything so that you never really have to think about it.

One of the bigger areas of concern for people is when it comes to finding their day-to-day things like keys, phones, and their purse or wallet.

The way to take control of that situation is to create a landing zone just inside the door you enter through the most often. A landing zone usually consists of a table where you can dump the mail into a basket, your keys into a bowl and leave your phone chargers so that you can charge your phones there overnight.

Book bags and purses can simply be tossed under the table for safe keeping. If you have enough space under the table, you can keep a pair of frequently worn shoes there as well. With a landing zone, you can quickly find those things you need every day.

RULES FOR SUCCESS:

1. When you find things throughout the house that belong at your landing zone, move those items there pronto.

Chapter 20:
Denial

"Sometimes your heart needs more time to accept what your mind already knows."

– Unknown

Many times we hold on to things that represent people or a time in our life that we're not ready to let go of or say goodbye to. By holding on to the items, we have constant reminders of that great time or person, which allows us to continue to put off dealing with the emotions connected to the realities at hand.

You're getting older and no longer have a purpose

We tend to keep our grown children's things from when they were smaller as a reminder of our youth as well as theirs. Their stuff reminds us of a happier time, a time when they needed us and showered us with unconditional love on a regular basis.

We hold on to the stuff from their childhood to avoid the feelings that come along with admitting that they have grown up and no longer need us to that degree. We hold on to their stuff to avoid having to accept that not only have they gotten older, so have we. When they were smaller, we knew what our role and purpose was. Many times when children grow up, we lose our identity because we no longer understand what our purpose or role is.

CLUTTER TRUTH #40:

If your grown children don't live with you, neither should their stuff.

Storing things for people that don't live with you is a big no-no. Of course there are crisis situations where you may temporarily store things for others. But as a general rule, if someone isn't living with you, their stuff shouldn't be living with you either.

Not ready to say goodbye

We keep things that we loved, things that represented different parts of our past and belongings of a loved one who has died because we're not ready to say goodbye to that thing, that time period or that person. We may not be ready to face the loss or what feels like them abandoning us. If we hold on to their stuff, then we feel like a part of them or that time period is still with us and we can put off feeling the enormity of the loss and all of the emotions and feelings that come with saying goodbye completely. Many times we're afraid that we'll forget them if we don't hold on to their things and we don't want to do that!

While I was getting dressed one day, I grabbed a bottle of my favorite perfume from the cabinet. When I noticed there were only a couple of squirts left, I put it back in the cabinet without using it. That's when it hit me. I had been doing the same thing over and over without realizing it. I was guilty of doing exactly what I coach many clients not to do.

You see, without realizing it, I had taken that same perfume bottle out with the intention of using it over and over for the last few years. Each time I was reminded that there were only a few squirts left, I would return it to the cabinet without using it.

Why would I say that this example has to do with denial? It's because that bottle of perfume was my all-time favorite perfume. I had worn it for years and had always gotten compliments on it. I loved it! To my dismay, they stopped making that perfume in 2004. Needless to say, I was thrilled to death when I found my current bottle in one of those airport perfume stores. I wore it every day until I got down to these last two squirts. That was probably in 2006 or so!

When I stopped and thought about what I had been doing with the perfume day after day, I realized that I was putting off using the last two squirts because then I would have to admit that it was gone and that I could never wear it again or buy any more.

Even worse, I would have to acknowledge that I have to go shopping for a new perfume. As I mentioned previously, I detest shopping. Here's the funny and ironic part though – I wasn't using the last two squirts because I didn't want to admit that it was gone and that I wouldn't be able to wear it every day. Yet I had already not been wearing it every day for the last four years as a result of trying to avoid using up the last two squirts! Can you relate to this story?

Not ready to admit that you've gained weight

When we unexpectedly gain weight, we have a tendency to hold on to the clothes that we *used to* be able to fit into, in the hopes that we can wear them again. While it's true that some of us will lose the new-found weight, a greater majority of us won't. However, we hold on to our smaller-size clothes because we don't want to accept and admit to ourselves that we've gained weight and probably won't be able to fit back into that size again.

We also hold on to the clothes we've outgrown because we may not want to acknowledge that we *really don't* have many clothes that fit us anymore. If we purged the clothes that no longer fit, we wouldn't be able to deny that we didn't have many clothes that fit us anymore. Then, we'd be forced into spending money buying new clothes – money that we may very well not have. It feels easier to pretend that you have lots of clothes, or that you're miraculously going to drop the extra pounds in a couple of weeks.

It's important that your closet is filled 100% with clothing that makes you feel and look great. You deserve to feel your best every single day!

Can't pay your bills

Before I began my work as a certified professional organizer, I had no idea that there was an enormous amount of people who avoid opening their mail like it's the plague! Many of the reasons they put off opening the mail have to do with denial.

When you are faced with opening bills that you can't pay, you feel like a failure. If you open the bills, then you have to worry about how you will pay them. Or worse yet, what will happen if you don't pay them? If you don't open the bills, you can erase all of that worry, and you can deny that you really owe them and can't afford to pay them.

You may not be opening the mail because you already feel pretty beat up in life and realize that if you did, it would just create more work and stress than you're ready to deal with at the moment. So instead, you choose to ignore it.

It's a spatial thing

One of the most obvious things we try to deny is the fact that we have more stuff than our space will allow. As long as you continue to deny this, your space will never feel peaceful or useful. Regardless of whether you decide to keep everything in your home or office, if you have more stuff than your space will allow, you simply cannot keep it all and think that you can keep things organized and functional.

CLUTTER TRUTH #41:

Clutter and disorganization cannot be solved simply by acquiring bins and tubs.

Very often people approach clutter and disorganization as a space problem that can be solved by acquiring bins and tubs rather than tackling the excess. (It's easier and more fun to go buy pretty tubs and containers than to go through our stuff!) Without realizing it, they are only adding to their clutter with the additional organizing products they purchase.

It's your turn...

FOOD FOR THOUGHT:

"The more things you own, the more they own you."
– Chuck Palahniuk

ACTION STEP:

Use these three tips to make your decluttering time more productive.

1. Set a specific block of time aside for decluttering.
2. Avoid leaving the room you're working in and becoming distracted elsewhere by putting things that belong in another room by the door with a note of where they go. When your decluttering time is up, move those piles to the area they belong.
3. Create a to-do list of things you find that you want or need to do as you go. Group the things that go with those to-do's together in one place. You may have things you want to return, clothes to try on, a picture to hang and so on.

RULES FOR SUCCESS:

1. Use black bags for trash and white bags for donations.
2. Systematically work through the room from left to right, leaving no surface unturned.

Chapter 21:
"I'm Gonna"™

"Insanity is doing the same thing over and over again and expecting different results."

– Albert Einstein, Physicist and Scientist

This is one of my all-time favorite excuses for holding on to unwanted or unneeded stuff. And it's probably the one that I hear the most often! If I had a dime for every time someone said *"I'm gonna"* do such and such with that item I'm holding on to, I'd be a millionaire! The list of things that we're *"gonna"* do is endless! I will go out on a limb here and say that I bet each and every one of us is guilty of using this phrase more than once in our lives. (I've been *"gonna"* write this book for years!)

My hope is that after you have read this book, you will catch yourself every time you say *"I'm gonna,"* and then you will take a few more minutes to think through if you are really ever *gonna* do it or not. Just becoming aware of the numerous times you say *"I'm gonna"* should help you to see why nine times out of ten, you probably really won't do it because you will realize you don't have enough time to do all of the things you say you're *gonna* do. Or you will realize you have other, more pressing things to do with your valuable time.

Good intentions

When we say *"I'm gonna"* do something, it normally comes from a good intention. We truly believe we're going to do it. The problem with the *"I'm gonna"* excuse is that your good intentions have to be matched with follow-through action and enough available time to do all of the things you say you're *"gonna"* do. Otherwise, all your *"I'm gonna"* excuses are doing nothing more than taking up space in your brain, your home or your office.

CLUTTER TRUTH #42:

Take a more realistic look at your *"I'm gonna's"* ™.

We're all brimming over with great plans and ideas, aren't we? What we tend to forget when we say *"I'm gonna"* is that we are limited by how much time or money we can invest doing these great things. We tend to not even realize how many times we've said *"I'm gonna."* The next time you catch yourself saying *"I'm gonna,"* really think through how much time and money you have available. If you don't have enough time or money to complete it, you must accept that and let it go, or determine what other thing you are willing to give up in order to pursue it.

Eventually we have to slow down long enough to make a rational decision about whether or not we'll really ever find the time or energy to do those things that are on our *"I'm gonna"* list. If we decide that we want to do something badly enough, we will have to carve out the time and energy to really DO IT, which may mean putting off other things we want to do more. We may also have to admit to ourselves that although we really want to do something, we are not ever *gonna* get around to doing it. And that's OK.

Does the *"I'm gonna"* ™ match the action?

As I mentioned before, if your good intentions aren't matched with follow-through action and the time to take that action, your *"I'm gonna"* list is just simply taking up space in your brain. It is important that you compare what you *say* you are *gonna* do with an item to what you are *really* doing with it.

Once you're clear about what you are *gonna* do with something you are keeping, it's important to be sure that you really do what you said you were *gonna* do with it. If you say you're keeping 20 issues of a magazine you love because you're *gonna* read them, then you should be taking steps to carve out the time to read them NOW, not down the road sometime. If you're keeping 25 old t-shirts because you're gonna make a t-shirt quilt out of them, you should be taking steps to have that done NOW, not down the road sometime.

A stay-at-home mom with two small children who kept her extremely busy, Elizabeth had lost complete control of her home office. It was covered wall-to-wall with paper piles. Every flat surface, including the floor, was littered with paperwork. She didn't know where anything was and she didn't know where to even begin to tackle things.

Working together, we sifted through all of the paperwork in the office. Taking the time to talk through the relevance of holding on to each item in detail helped Elizabeth make good decisions about whether or not she should continue to keep it or let it go.

During the process, we came across dozens of her husband's paycheck stubs that she had kept throughout the year. When I asked her why she was keeping them, she said that she was holding on to them because she was "gonna" match them up with the year-end statement to be sure that it was correct.

While I felt that she could have easily just kept the most current paycheck stub after confirming that the totals were transferring over properly from the last paycheck, I thought she gave a valid reason for keeping them, and so I didn't push the issue of letting them go further.

However, about three hours into going through her paperwork, we came across the year-end statement. The minute she saw the year-end statement she said, "OK, we can toss those paycheck stubs now because I have the year-end statement." And with that, she began shredding the stubs.

What I want you to notice is that although she said she was keeping the paycheck stubs to compare to the year-end statement, she didn't compare the year-end statement with the stubs to be sure it was correct at all! Instead, she simply began shredding all of the paycheck stubs she had saved without ever attempting to compare them to the statement.

Obviously, her "I'm gonna" reason for keeping the items wasn't valid or accurate. So there was no reason to keep the paycheck stubs because she never looked back at them like she said she was "gonna" do – her "I'm gonna" didn't match the action she took.

Does your *"I'm gonna"* ™ have a deadline?

If you take the time to think through the importance of your *"I'm gonna"* and the time it will take to complete it, and you still decide that you really are *"gonna"* do that thing, it's imperative that you give yourself a deadline to complete that action. We have so many things on our never-ending to-do lists that we can't realistically get to all of them. Giving yourself deadlines forces you to look at everything you want to do more realistically.

CLUTTER TRUTH #43:

Lean into action.

If you feel immobilized at the thought of something you have to do, don't think about everything you have to do to complete whatever it is. Instead, simply move in the direction of taking action. If you want to declutter your garage but the entire space is filled with stuff, look for the easiest thing you can do at the moment. That may be to remove all empty cardboard boxes and recycle them. Or it may be to dry out your left-over paint so you can dispose of it. Just *do something* regardless of how small it may seem in the big picture. Then repeat.

Vivica struggled with clutter her entire life. Not only was her entire home taken over by clutter, she also had a couple of storage units filled with treasures she had acquired. The enormous amount of clutter in her bedroom had prevented her from sleeping in her bed for years.

Working our way through the stuff in her bedroom, we finally made our way to the closet. As we sorted through things one by one, we talked through each item in detail in order to help her make decisions about whether or not she should keep it or let it go. We talked about how each item looked, how it fit, how it made her feel when she wore it, etc.

Since the rest of Vivica's house was so cluttered you could barely walk through it, we spent a lot of time talking about how it would be impossible for her to keep every piece of clothing she had because there was not enough space to store all of them. I had to keep reminding her that if she continued to keep everything, she would never be able to reach her goal of sleeping in her bed again.

While going through her clothes, we came across three different garments that she insisted she wanted to keep because she loved them so much that she was "gonna" repair them. As a certified professional organizer with a lot of experience working with clients, I knew the chances of that ever happening were very slim. Working on decluttering was challenging enough for her and had been a very slow process. With our big-picture focus being on digging out from under her extremely cluttered situation, I knew it was going to be quite a while before she got back to the smaller details of repairing those three garments, if she ever got to that at all.

As a professional though, my job is to help guide and coach people into making their own good, well-though-out decisions. So even though I knew that the items needing repair were most likely going to end up buried under her clutter again, I couldn't force my opinion on her. Instead, I put those three garments in a plastic shopping bag that I tied closed. I taped a DATED note on the bag that said "I'm gonna" repair these items.

I explained to Vivica that I dated her "I'm gonna" so that when she came across it later, she would realize how long she had been saying she was "gonna" do it. My hope is that when she finds that bag at the bottom of her closet again many, many years from now, she'll see the dated note on it, smile as she remembers our conversation and realize that she's not really "gonna" get to it. At that point, my hope is that she should have no further hesitations about letting them go.

Good intentions vs. reality

We talked about how all clutter represents delayed decisions in Chapter 16 and we talked about how your *"I'm gonna"* excuse is based on good intentions in this chapter. If your good intentions aren't matched with action, they remain simply good intentions.

As we've discussed in this book, making decisions about whether to keep or let go of our stuff is hard work because it can trigger memories and emotions that we would prefer to avoid. Because of that, we delay making decisions on our stuff, which results in clutter piling up.

Without realizing it, saying *"I'm gonna"* is a sneaky way of continuing to put off making a decision. It allows you to fall back on the good intention of what you plan to do with that item, rather than facing the reality. *"I'm gonna"* is the perfect statement to make when we want to delay the reality of what is really going on. We use this statement to ignore the truth and blur the cold, hard facts in front of us.

Here are a few *"I'm gonna"* excuses, along with the reality of how each represents delaying a decision.

GOOD INTENTION   vs. REALITY

"I'm gonna" return it.	Just saying you're going to return it without taking any action to make that a reality is simply a good intention. If you're going to return it, the action that should follow that statement is to bag it up, locate the receipt and get it in your car.
"I'm gonna" recycle it.	Just saying you're going to recycle it without taking any action to make that a reality is simply a good intention. If you're going to recycle something, it should be moved to the area where you keep recycling until it's picked up.

GOOD INTENTION vs. REALITY

"I'm gonna" give that to a friend.	Just saying you're going to give it to a friend without taking any action to make that a reality is simply a good intention. If you're going to give it to a friend, bag it up, put a label on it with your friend's name, hang it on the front door and add it to your to-do list.
"I'm gonna" read it.	Does the amount of time you have available to read match the amount of reading you want to do? If you subscribe to five or six magazines, in addition to all of the books you want to read, but you only have one or two hours a month to sit still and read, then this statement is not realistic.
"I'm gonna" fix it.	In this day and age of disposable everything, have you thought through whether or not you would really take the time and energy to fix the broken thing you have, instead of running out and buying a new one when you need it?

155

GOOD INTENTION vs. REALITY

"I'm gonna" make this.	If you copy or clip recipes frequently because you love to cook, or better yet, because you want to cook again someday, does the amount of recipes you have gathered match the number of times you find yourself looking for a new recipe? If not, this behavior is allowing you to delay more decisions. Take the time to think through whether you will *really* ever use the recipes as you think you will.

CLUTTER TRUTH #44:

Compare and prioritize your *"I'm gonna's"* ™.

If you're still holding on to more *"I'm gonna's"* than you have available time or money to invest in, an effective way to let go of more of them is to compare them with one another. This exercise helps you to see which things are really most meaningful to you. When you take the time to prioritize your *"I'm gonna's"* and can readily see the most important ones, it's easier to identify and let go of the ones that don't matter as much.

Taking the time to go through our clutter and release the things that no longer serve a purpose in our lives is such a freeing experience. The same holds true when you re-examine all of your *"I'm gonna's"* and release the ones that you realize aren't really important enough to you to make the time to do them.

It's your turn...

FOOD FOR THOUGHT:

"Nothing is so fatiguing as the eternal hanging on of an uncompleted task." – William James

ACTION STEP:

1. Look back over the list of *"I'm gonna's,"* both the good intention and the reality, and see if there are any that you can identify with.
2. If there is, ask yourself the hard questions.
   a. Am I really going to do that?
   b. Do I really have enough time to do this?
   c. Are there other things I enjoy doing more that would cause me to put this *"I'm gonna"* off even longer?
3. If after careful examination you find that you probably won't get to that specific *"I'm gonna,"* allow yourself the grace to let it go.

RULES FOR SUCCESS:

1. Don't blur the truth as you make these decisions.
2. Think about the things you love to do while you look through the various *"I'm gonna's."* Use the things you love to do as a gauge against whether or not you would choose to do the *"I'm gonna"* over doing those things you love doing. This will help you to determine how important each one really is.

Chapter 22:
The Freeing Power of Letting Go

"Once we give up being attached to physical possessions, we find the time and freedom to follow bigger dreams."

– Joshua Becker, Author

We've talked about how clutter is caused by delayed decisions and about how it negatively impacts your life and prevents you from experiencing a more fulfilling and satisfying life. ***Now we get to focus a little time on the best part – the freeing power of letting go,*** and the opportunity you have to make a significant, positive impact on someone else's life with your unwanted stuff.

It can feel scary, even overwhelming, to you to begin to sort through your belongings, looking at them with a different set of eyes, and thinking through why you *really* have them. But I promise you it becomes so much easier within a short time. Letting go feels like you just took a deep, cleansing breath of fresh air. Although it can be mentally exhausting to take the time to go through your stuff, it is also very freeing, eye-opening and addictive.

Empowered and motivated

As you begin facing your clutter head on and making decisions about the value each item brings, or doesn't bring, to your life, you start to feel more in control of your surroundings, which in turn makes you feel more in control of your life. This process leaves you feeling empowered about your life and motivated to continue taking back control.

CLUTTER TRUTH #45:

Getting organized helps you feel more in control of your life and future!

When your surroundings are chaotic and out of control, your life feels out of control. Taking the time to declutter and get organized helps you to become clearer on what's important to you as you weed out the unnecessary stuff in your life. Establishing what's most important to you helps you to live a more intentional, focused life.

Peaceful and less stress

As you make decisions on the value that unwanted and/or unnecessary items bring to your life, and you watch them begin to leave your space, you will immediately start feeling more peaceful as you see the space opening up. Since you are no longer enslaved or controlled by the constant chatter of your things, or weighed down by all of the decisions you've put off, you will notice a marked reduction in your stress level.

Increase in confidence

As your life and your spaces are freed from all of the excess and unnecessary items that weren't bringing any value to your life, you will notice an increase in overall confidence. That increase can be attributed to the fact that your life and your spaces are no longer full of the constant negative talk and lies from clutter.

Increased productivity and efficiency

Once you are surrounded only by the things that support your life or work, your productivity and efficiency will increase because you will no longer be constantly distracted by the chatter of unfinished things clamoring for your attention.

Save time, money and energy

There are a number of our clients who initially say they can't really afford our services. And then, in the first session or two they are jumping for joy and praising us for the amount of money we saved them, or found for them. You really do save money when you get organized!

It's a well-known fact, and something I touched on in Chapter 9, when you have too much stuff and aren't organized, it costs you not only money, but also time and energy. When you let go of the things that aren't serving any purpose in your life, you will undoubtedly have less stuff.

With less stuff, it's much easier to organize and find homes for things so that you *can* find them when you need them and you don't waste time or energy searching for them or redoing them (i.e., grocery list, business report, etc.). Your energy level increases because you are no longer drained by all of the delayed decisions and constant chatter and lies from your clutter.

You also won't continue to spend money replacing things that you already have but can't find, or things that are damaged, in the mass of clutter. When your things are organized, you're more likely to have a plan in place for routine maintenance, which will help prevent the need to pay much larger repair bills because things weren't properly maintained (car, heating and cooling, etc.).

After Felicia and her husband divorced, she continued to raise their two boys alone while working and attending college full-time. Without an extra second to spare, the clutter quickly piled up in their family home. Still struggling with the emotions and unresolved issues from her divorce, the added stress and chaos from the excessive clutter left her feeling defeated at all times.

Her entire home, basement and garage had been taken over with so much stuff that it made even walking through the home very difficult. With all of that clutter and disorganization surrounding her at all times, her entire life felt out of control. One by one, the kids grew up and moved out. With these losses came depression.

One of Felicia's problem areas was processing and managing her mail and paperwork. There were papers and unopened mail everywhere! As a result of her losing control in this area, she was paying enormous amounts in late charges and bounced check fees. Utility companies frequently threatened disconnection – and even disconnected a time or two. When that happened, reconnection charges were also applied and many times she would have to take time off work for the services to be reconnected.

After working together on this issue, she was surprised to find that the problem wasn't that she didn't have enough money to pay her bills – the problem was that since things were so out of control, she spent all of her time and energy focused on putting out fires. Working together, we set up a specific day each week to process her paperwork and pay bills. We straightened out her bank account and check register, and set up a budget so that she'd know exactly when each bill was due.

Within just a matter of months, we were able to easily see how much money she was saving using this approach because she was no longer paying late charges, bad check fees and reconnection charges. She was shocked to find that she always had a lot of money left over after paying her bills. She had no idea that she really had plenty of money to pay her bills the whole time because she had lost control of the situation many, many years earlier. Not only is she saving money now, her stress is reduced and she's not wasting so much energy on putting out fires.

Space opens for wonderful stuff to come in

Once you've cleared the decks of all of the unnecessary physical (and mental) stuff that is clogging up your life, it opens up space for new, wonderful stuff to come in! As I hope I've explained in this book, in addition to physical space, clutter takes up a lot of mental space as well. When your mind and space are free of all the negative mental and physical traps connected with clutter, you have more room for a fuller life filled with new, wonderful experiences, relationships and abundance.

Since you are no longer constantly distracted by memories of your past, lost loved ones, your failures and so on and so forth, you can focus on the here and now and your future. Focusing on the present moment and your future allows prosperity, abundance and blessings to come in.

Melanie and her two-year-old son were forced to move back in with her parents after her recent divorce. Except for a few bigger items, the majority of their belongings were shoved into the two bedrooms they had in her parents' home.

Not only was Melanie a single parent now, she was also attending school and running a small business. She called me for help because she was having trouble concentrating with all of the clutter surrounding her. (Remember, clutter is ALWAYS talking to you.)

One of her struggles was paperwork, so we created a system that streamlined that for her, but her biggest problem area was baby stuff. When her son was born, she received lots of clothes and baby gear from her family and friends. Although her son couldn't use any of the baby stuff anymore, she held on to all of it, just in case she had another little boy down the road.

A big part of a professional organizer's job is coaching people to help them make realistic decisions about their stuff, and this situation was no different. We began by talking about how she didn't have a need to keep the stuff for another child she might have. We then moved on to the fact that she probably wouldn't be having a child anytime soon since she was recently divorced and wasn't even dating anyone new yet. We talked about the many places she could donate the stuff where it would be used to help people that really needed it.

Once we talked it through in great detail, she easily made the decision to let it go. She was able to see that she didn't have a practical need to continue holding on to the stuff. She realized that holding on to it was having a negative impact on her current life and that, if she chose to let go of it, she could bless someone who was in pain because they needed it so much.

Taking the time to declutter and get organized opened up space for something new and wonderful to come in. Within a few months of our work together, she met someone, fell madly in love and remarried. Here's the icing on the cake... he came complete with two small children of his own.

The joy of helping others

As much as your unwanted stuff has been a burden to you, it could be a real blessing to someone in need! If you're still having trouble tackling your clutter, I hope that by knowing how much your unwanted stuff could help others, you will be motivated to take action and get started. There are so many really great ministries, charities and families out there in desperate need of your stuff. If you won't take the time to declutter for yourself, please do it for others. You really do have the power to make a positive impact in someone's life with your unwanted stuff. And you'll get to feel the joy of helping others in return – in addition to the benefits of freeing up your own space!

I have been a single mom since my daughters were 3 years old and 6 months old. Sadly, my children's father, his family and my extended family were not financially or actively involved in the kids' lives after we divorced. Long story short, I was doing it all alone – physically, emotionally and financially.

Even though I had always worked full-time and had a good job, most of my salary was eaten up by daycare costs. That sounds so cliché, but our reality was that daycare costs left very little money for anything else, including food. I ate popcorn for what seemed like every meal so that I could feed the kids. I juggled money to pay our utilities and rent.

At one point, my car engine blew up. It was going to cost $2,000 to fix it. I did not have $2,000 or anywhere to turn for the money. So for seven months, my daughters and I lived without a car and without any help. Every day for those seven months I would walk my children to daycare, carrying the baby, the diaper bag and my purse, while holding my oldest daughter's hand as she walked – that is, when she did not demand that I carry her too. It did not matter if it was raining, snowing or sunny, we did this every day for seven months. (Imagine trying to hold an umbrella on those rainy days!) From there, I would catch a bus and make the long one-hour commute to work downtown. Every night I would catch the same bus back to daycare, and then we would walk home.

While we had a place to call home, we had little else. All we had in the living room of our small apartment was a love seat, nothing else, just a love seat. Ironically, during this same time period, I overheard a co-worker complaining that she was so stressed out by all of the stuff she had in her basement. It was driving her crazy! She complained that her two-year-old daughter already had a TV and VCR in her room and she still had two or three more in the basement. I was shocked! How could that be possible when all we had in our living room was a love seat?!

My heart sank as I listened. I would have been humiliated for her to know this, but all I could think of was how much I could have used her stuff. I was fascinated by the fact that although we were on two very different ends of the "stuff" spectrum, excess "stuff" or lack of "stuff" was causing both of us so much pain!

Little did I know that 15 years later I would launch Simplified Living Solutions, Inc., a professional organizing company that helps people through the agony of dealing with too much stuff. Most of the time when people finally work up the nerve to call my company for help, they are more than ready to let go of their stuff, which is a good thing. The bad thing is that they want their stuff gone NOW!

Early in my professional organizing career, I realized that many of our clients would end up with half of their household belongings at the curb waiting to be picked up as trash because that is the easiest and fastest way to get it out of their lives. Many times, items still had tags on them, were barely used and were still in great condition. My heart would ache for the people who could have used that stuff but could not afford to buy it themselves. I was haunted by the fact that I was playing a part in filling our landfills with usable stuff that could have helped others.

As a result of this experience and a passion to see the gap bridged between the two groups, I created a FREE nationwide website, The Stuff Stop (www.TheStuffStop.com), whose purpose is to help people match up their unwanted stuff with people in need. The Stuff Stop connects you with ministries and charities in your area that will take your unwanted stuff and use it to help others. Can you see how much power we have to make a positive impact in the lives of others, simply by allowing the excess stuff we do not need to be used by someone who does need it? It feels so great to help others!

You can make a difference in someone's life, and I believe, in the world by being purposeful about the stuff you buy, consume and discard. Not only are we using up our natural resources at record speed and destroying our earth by filling up landfills with our unwanted stuff, we are missing the power we have to help and empower others in need with the unwanted stuff that is clogging up our lives.

It's your turn...

FOOD FOR THOUGHT:

"You can't reach for anything new if your hands are still full of yesterday's junk." – Louise Smith

ACTION STEP:

1. For the next 30 days, find at least one item that you are willing to let go of.
2. Purposefully think about who might need that item or who it could help.
3. If you can't think of a personal connection that could use the item, research ministries and charities that might have a use for it. If it's old blankets or linens, an animal shelter would love those. If it's unused makeup, a home for troubled young women would be happy to take it.
4. Take action to get those items to their new owners.
5. Take some time to reflect on how great it feels to connect your unwanted stuff with people who are in need of it. This will help you to stay motivated to continue tackling your stuff.

RULES FOR SUCCESS:

1. Be intentional!

Chapter 23:
Declutter and Discover Your Dreams!

"The best way to find out what we really need is to get rid of what we don't."

– Marie Kondō, Author

In *The Success Principles*™, author Jack Canfield recommends hiring a professional organizer to help you clean up your messes and your incomplete projects to make space for something new. Implementing the steps shared in this chapter, and the tips sprinkled throughout the book, will help you regain control of your life and surroundings and take powerful steps toward creating the life of your dreams!

Few realize that we have the power to live the life of our dreams, rather than just being stuck with the life we feel we've been dealt. Our lives are made up of *daily decisions* on how we will spend our time, money and energy. Without goals or an idea of what we want, we simply move from one thing to the next without much thought or passion on our part. With goals and clarity about what is important to us, our life has purpose and meaning. It's difficult to have this kind of clarity when you are surrounded by clutter and chaos.

Step 1: Know that you deserve it

This is a hard one for many of us. We've been led to believe in various ways throughout our lives that we don't deserve happiness, joy or abundance. Many were taught that it's selfish to put our needs first. Some of us spend our days beating ourselves up over past mistakes.

Would you believe me if I told you that your attitude about all of this is a choice? It is. You *DO* deserve happiness, joy and abundance. If you don't put your needs before others and take care of yourself, no one else will. If you're not healthy and happy, you can't take care of those people and things around you that need your attention.

Step 2: Determine what your vision is

It's important that you take some time beforehand to get clear on your vision, values and purpose. You'll need to know the overall vision you have for your life. Determining your vision consists of answering these questions:

- What do you want out of life?
- What is important to you?
- What really matters in your life?

I believe we were all put here for a very specific reason and purpose. We each have a message. What is yours?

When it comes to getting organized and decluttering, you'll need to be clear on your vision for the space that you'll be working on. Determining your vision for the space consists of answering these questions:

- How do you want to use the area?
- What kind of things do you want to do in this area?

Once you know what you want to do in the space, it will be easier to see what belongs (and what doesn't belong) in that space. If you don't know how you want to use the space or what your vision for it is yet, start off by determining what you want less of in that space.

Your vision may be to take a clutter-filled room and transform it into a fun place for the kids to hang out in, play games and watch TV. Or your vision may be to transform a guest room into a home office where you can use your computer, pay bills and create products. Notice how each vision not only addresses the purpose of the space, but it specifies the activities you want to do as well.

Step 3: Break your vision down into manageable pieces

Once you have determined what your vision or goal is for organizing an area of your life or a physical space, it's important that you take the time to break down how to reach that vision in manageable bite-size pieces to avoid feeling apprehensive or worried at the thought of tackling it.

Just making the decision to lose 30 pounds doesn't help you to reach that goal unless you take the additional time and energy needed to break down the necessary steps to get there. You can't go from drinking sugary sodas and eating fast food for every meal to drinking water and cooking well-balanced meals overnight. It takes time. Every internal and external change takes mental preparation and a plan.

Step one might be that you decide to keep your focus on getting healthy rather than losing weight so that your routine doesn't feel so strict. Step two might be to replace one soda a day with water. Step three might be to cook one well-balanced meal a day. Step four might be to work your way down to one soda a day. Step five might be to figure out how to start counting calories and so on.

If your goal was to declutter and organize your kitchen, step one might be to clear the table top of all of the excess. Step two might be to sort through your dishes and purge the ones you no longer use. Step three might be to go through the food and toss anything that is expired or that you no longer enjoy. Step four might be to go through your cleaning supplies and consolidate the duplicates and toss the ones you don't use.

Step 4: Take action and make decisions

Don't live life stuck in the *"I'm gonna"* stage. Your life is here and now, and the moments are fleeting! The daily choices we make, combined with the actions we take, change the course of our lives. It's time to **take action** to get the clutter out of your life as a first step toward creating the life of your dreams.

Keeping in mind that *all clutter* represents delayed decisions, the best way to take action is to begin making those decisions. It's much easier to make those decisions and choices once you know what your vision is. Remember that you should keep only those things that you need, use or love. Let go of things that aren't moving you closer to your goals and vision.

Step 5: Reward yourself

It's imperative that you set up a reward system to keep your motivation going. Don't get too caught up on what your reward might be. It doesn't have to be anything elaborate. However, I would say that for now, your reward should not be shopping since you are focusing on sending things out, not bringing things in.

A reward can be as simple as a nice, hot shower after getting all sweaty from cutting the grass and doing yard work. Knowing your reward is a nice, hot shower should motivate you to finish cutting the grass and doing all of the yard work so that you can get in the shower now, rather than later if you drag it out.

For me, I love nothing more than an ice cold tea from my favorite local gas station. I've used this as my reward so many times in life. When I was dieting, I would reward myself with a tea after forcing myself to drink tons of water the first half of the day. When I was swimming to get in shape, I would reward myself with a tea after I swam. I reward myself with a tea after a long day of helping someone get organized that proved to be extremely physically demanding.

As you can see, there are all sorts of ways to use the same reward in a variety of different ways. Take a minute to figure out what your reward(s) will be and write them down.

CLUTTER TRUTH #48:

As you look through the things in your space, ask yourself questions like the ones listed below to help you fully process each item.

1. Do I *really* want this?
2. Do I *really* need this in my life right now?
3. Do I *really* use this?
4. Is this something *"I'm gonna"* do something with?
5. Am I really going to do it?
6. Does this *really* serve a purpose or fulfill a need in my life as it is now?
7. Does this move me *toward* my goals and vision?
8. Is it really worth my time to keep this?
9. Am I really doing what I think I am doing with this item?
10. Will I really do what I thought I would do with this item?
11. Is it worth keeping this item if it means I cannot use this space because it is all clogged up with stuff I am keeping *"just in case?"*

Step 6: Accept that backsliding is part of the process

As I mentioned before, you can't change your habits overnight. You also can't change everything at once. That's why it's so important to break your desired goals down into manageable bite-size pieces. Even doing that won't prevent backsliding, but it will make a dramatic impact on the outcome.

It takes time and determination to keep starting over where you left off when you backslide. Be patient with yourself. Remember that any steps you take or progress you make is better than no progress at all. It's so important that you are kind to yourself. Stay motivated by keeping your focus on what you *did do,* rather than what you *still have left to do.* This kind of thinking will help you get back on track much quicker than if you focus on what you have left to do.

It's your turn...

FOOD FOR THOUGHT:

"A goal without a plan is just a wish."
– Antoine de Saint-Exupery

ACTION STEP:

Mentally prepare yourself for change by asking yourself the following clarifying questions and seeing where they lead you.

1. What do you want more of in your life?
2. What do you want less of in your life?
3. What causes you the most stress?
4. What brings you the most happiness?
5. Think about the ways in which clutter negatively impacts your life.
6. Become more aware of the many times you're stressed out because you can't find what you are looking for.
7. Take notice of the amount of space you are forfeiting the use of because it is full of stuff.

RULES FOR SUCCESS:

1. After determining what is most important to you in your life, carve out space to make it happen.

Chapter 24:
The Keys to Success

"Shop deliberately. Shop thoughtfully.
Shop responsibly. Shop less."

– Katy Wolk-Stanley, Blogger

I hope that the information I've shared in this book has helped you to understand that in most cases, it is not the actual object that you are attached to, but rather it's the experience, memory or person that is connected with the item that causes you to cling so tightly to it. Letting go of the stuff you don't need won't make your memories any less precious, it will only make your life fuller! I hope that you feel empowered to let go of the stuff that has been holding you back, so that you can pursue life with a renewed sense of vigor and intention.

Have a plan and rules for your stuff

Having a plan and rules for your stuff is uber-important. It's OK to keep things *IF* you need, use or love them, as long as you have a plan for how you will manage them and you have the space to keep them. You'll need to know where the items will "live" in your space, in addition to what organizing product (if any) they will be stored in. You will also have to take the time to think through what the limits or rules are for each item.

For instance, you may designate a specific tub in your basement to store greeting cards because you have a hard time parting with them. The rule for your greeting cards might be that once that tub is full, you'll have to purge old ones that have lost their value before you can add any new ones.

Lorraine had so many newspaper and magazines subscriptions that they were taking over her entire household. No matter how much coaching we did, she wasn't ready to give up on the notion that she **could** *read everything she wanted to read – even though she could clearly see that the amount of time she had available to read didn't match the amount of stuff she wanted to read.*

In order to accommodate her decision to continue receiving ALL of her subscriptions, but to ensure that the unread stuff started going out, I created a system for her reading materials using four wall pockets. Each pocket represented three different months. The first pocket represented January, May and September. The second pocket represented February, June and October. The third pocket represented March, July and November. The fourth pocket represented April, August and December.

The plan was that as her reading materials arrived, she was to put them in the wall pocket that represented that month. By the time May rolled around, if she hadn't read the materials that were in the pocket from January, she had to recycle those to make room for her May reading to be stored in that wall pocket.

This system allowed her to hold on to the "I'm gonna" read-all-of-this excuse she had been using, but also kept things more under control by forcing her to move the old stuff out of the space. I am also confident that eventually this system helped her to realize that it would be impossible for her to read everything she wanted to. Armed with that information, my hope is that she eventually cancelled all of her subscriptions except for those that mattered most and that she had time to read.

CLUTTER TRUTH #49:
Label. Label. Label.

The importance of labeling things can't be stressed enough. Not only do labels help people know *where* things belong, they are also a reminder of what *doesn't* belong somewhere. You're more likely to toss random stuff in an unmarked tub than in a tub that clearly defines what belongs in it.

Weed constantly

Thanks to birthdays, holidays, mail, catalogs, magazines, newspapers, friends, family, children and spouses, it takes little or no effort for clutter to come into our lives. That's why we have to be ruthless about getting it out.

Our taste in things changes, and many things lose their value over time. It's important to revisit things every six to twelve months. You don't have to revisit everything in your house all at once; you can break it down. For instance, you can make a quick run through the things in your kitchen one month. The next month you can glance at the things in your bedroom and so on.

Continually working through your spaces (or other clutter problems as described in Chapter 1) breaks the task down for you so that it's more manageable and you revisit things more frequently. To create flow in your life, things must constantly be going out.

Make decisions *before* you bring things into your space or life

One way you can drastically cut down on the amount of clutter in your home or office is to think through every single purchase you make, *before you make it.* It is important to slow down and look at things long enough to really think through why you are buying them, if they will really serve the purpose you think they will, etc. It is amazing how many things we buy without thinking about it and how little we buy when we stop and ask ourselves the hard questions that will help us determine whether or not we really need the item.

You can make a difference in the world by being purposeful about the stuff you buy, consume and discard. If you don't need it, don't bring it into your space. Never buy or bring anything into your home or office that you haven't completely thought through. Make a conscious decision about everything you bring into your home, office or life *before* you bring it in. If you don't need it, don't think you'll use it or don't love it, don't bring it into your space.

CLUTTER TRUTH #50:

Make decisions about things *before* you bring them into your space.

Rather than allowing things to continue flowing freely into your house and making decisions about their relevance *after the fact*, approach things proactively by thoroughly thinking through everything you bring into your home *before* you bring it in.

It's very rare that I buy anything without thinking it all of the way through. Many times I stand in the store holding an item for a very long time while I think through in detail whether or not it will fit the need or purpose I have for it. If I'm still on the fence after doing all of that, but am leaning toward thinking I should get it, I'll buy it and bring it home so that I can think about it longer. However, I do not take it out of the box until I've completely convinced myself that I'll really use it. I place it somewhere that is in my way so that I have to continue my thought process rather than tucking it away in a basement or closet to be forgotten.

One time I went against my better judgment and set out to buy a quesadilla maker, even though I rarely cook. At that time, I had fallen in love with these wonderful chicken quesadillas that were served at a local restaurant – so much so, that I found myself going to the restaurant every other day because I loved them so much!

*I had decided that I could save a lot of money and time if I started making the quesadillas at home myself. It was that thought that motivated me to overlook the cold hard facts and buy it anyway. In reality, I knew it was a long shot that I would ever make them because of my busy lifestyle and the fact that I don't like to cook. So even though I really **wanted to** make them, I returned the quesadilla* *maker, knowing all too well that it would never happen.*

Do what you *should* be doing rather than what you *want* to be doing

The most obvious thing that any of us can do to keep clutter at bay is to do what we *should* be doing instead of what we *want* to be doing. Rather than sitting idly by hoping that something will miraculously get done on its own, get up and face it yourself. To build motivation, continually remind yourself that *you are* in charge of your destiny and that *you do* have the power, tenacity and discipline to take back control of your life and your space. Then take action.

If you want to lose weight but you continue to eat everything in sight because that's what you want to be doing, you won't reach your goal. You have to stop saying *"I'm gonna"* and get around to actually doing it.

A great way to motivate yourself to take action and do what you should be doing is to use the reward system mentioned in Chapter 23. Tell yourself that before you can do what you *want* to do, you have to do what you *should* be doing first. Then your reward for doing what you didn't want to do first is that you get to do what you did want to do later. (Clear as mud, right?)

Schedule uninterrupted time

A good overall time management skill is to schedule uninterrupted time to complete projects or tasks more effectively. The same holds true with decluttering and getting organized. Just as you would never pour a cake mix into a bowl and then return hours later to add the eggs and other ingredients, you can't tackle your clutter in a few minutes here and a few minutes there. You'll need to devote a specific amount of uninterrupted time toward the task. This is part of the reason that working with a professional organizer helps people, because they schedule a block of time on their calendar that is devoted to the project of getting organized.

It's your turn...

FOOD FOR THOUGHT:

"Success is the sum of small efforts,
repeated day in and day out."
– Robert Collier

ACTION STEP:

Ten tips to remember:

1. Keep only those things that you need, use or love.
2. Assign a home and a space limit for all of your belongings.
3. Weed constantly.
4. Be intentional in your purchases or acquiring.
5. Keep only a limited amount of your children's artwork.
6. Only keep paperwork that truly serves a purpose.
7. Take action to reduce or stop junk mail and email.
8. Reduce the number of *"I'm gonna's"* you have.
9. Sort like items with like items to better determine how much of any given item you have so that you can make better decisions about what to keep.
10. Consolidate things when you have multiples.

RULES FOR SUCCESS:

1. Be kind to yourself.
2. Take one step at a time.

Let's Connect

I would love to connect with you! Please feel free to contact me to share a success story, to ask a question, or for a boost of encouragement and motivation!

https://www.SimplifiedLivingSolutions.com

Facebook
Simplified Living Solutions, Inc.
(https://www.facebook.com/SimplifiedLivingSolutionsInc)

Twitter
Sue Anderson
(https://twitter.com/SueAnderson)

LinkedIn
Sue Anderson, SLS
(https://www.linkedin.com/in/sueandersonsls)

Pinterest
Simplified Living Solutions
(https://www.pinterest.com/SLSOrganizing/)

YouTube
Simplified Living Solutions, Inc.
(https://www.youtube.com/user/SueAndersonSLS)

Not Sure What to Do with Your Unwanted Stuff?

Visit The Stuff Stop at www.TheStuffStop.com

The Stuff Stop is *the place* to turn to when you're ready to dispose of those things that you no longer need, use or love in a responsible, green way that helps people in need at the same time!

It's a **FREE** nationwide community resource website that provides information to match up your unwanted stuff with local charities, ministries and companies that will connect it with people in need.

Information is also provided that will enable you to recycle or dispose of your unwanted stuff in a green way rather than having it end up in a landfill.

Facebook
(https://www.facebook.com/TheStuffStop)

Twitter
(https://twitter.com/TheStuffStop)

Pinterest
(https://www.pinterest.com/thestuffstop/)

YouTube
(https://www.youtube.com/user/thestuffstop)

About the Author

"Bottom line, nothing makes me happier than helping, encouraging and empowering others. It is both humbling and rewarding to be chosen to play a part in making a positive change in others' lives."

–Sue Anderson, Certified Professional Organizer

Sue Anderson, a Certified Professional Organizer (CPO®) and President of Simplified Living Solutions, is an expert in the professional organizing field who specializes in clutter control, whole house transformations, downsizing, unpacking and paper management.

As a result of her natural ability to "see" how things could fit better, flow better or work more efficiently, combined with her authentic passion and strong desire to help others achieve peace, simplicity and order in their lives by getting organized, she founded Simplified Living Solutions, Inc., a professional organizing company, in 2007.

Sue believes that clutter and disorganization stop people from living life to its fullest potential by keeping them in a constant state of distraction. She loves playing a part in empowering people to be all they can be by giving them back control of their homes, offices and lives.

A self-professed "organizing maniac," she has been helping family and friends get organized her entire life – *whether they wanted it or not!* She loves the thrill of empowering busy people who are overwhelmed by their chaotic environments by creating solutions for a better, simpler life for them! Working with clients hands-on and teaching them how to effectively manage their time, tasks and stuff, she helps them to set up their homes, offices and lives so that they function more efficiently and effortlessly.

Understanding the stigma and shame associated with being disorganized, Sue uses her natural, nonjudgmental ability to put people at ease right away. She can easily see past the chaos at hand and visualize the clutter-free and organized end result. Using her creative problem-solving skills, along with her innate understanding of organization, she creates personalized systems that make daily processes flow more smoothly and efficiently. Tackling chaotic and stressful areas and transforming them into functional, peaceful spaces is FUN and EXCITING for Sue! *"The bigger the mess, the more I love the work!"* she says.

As one of only a few hundred professional organizers nationwide who have earned the credential of Certified Professional Organizer (CPO), Sue is recognized as an expert in the professional organizing field and is among those who are on the leading edge of education and standards concerning the organizing industry. She has appeared on KSDK, KPLR, KMOV, FOX2, KMOX, "Today in St Louis" and "Great Day St Louis," in addition to being featured in the *Suburban Journal* and *St Louis Spaces*. Simplified Living Solutions was chosen as the #1 Professional Organizing Company in St Louis by *St. Louis at Home* magazine.

I would be honored if you would be willing to take a moment and leave a review for my book on Amazon! And, I would appreciate it if you'd be willing to share my book with your family and friends.

Sue